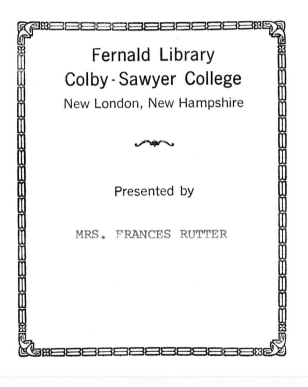

CULTURAL FOUNDATIONS OF
INDUSTRIAL CIVILIZATION

CULTURAL FOUNDATIONS OF INDUSTRIAL CIVILIZATION

BY

JOHN U. NEF

Chairman, Committee on Social Thought
and Professor of Economic History in the
University of Chicago

Archon Books
1974

Library of Congress Cataloging in Publication Data

Nef, John Ulric, 1899-
    Cultural foundations of industrial civilization.

    Reprint of the 1958 ed. published at the University Press,
Cambridge, which was issued as 1956 of The Wiles lectures.
    Includes bibliographical references.
    1. Technology   and   civilization.   2. Civilization—His-
tory.   I. Title.   II. Series: The Wiles lectures, 1956.
CB478.N4 1974   901.93   73-13742
ISBN 0-208-01406-3

First published 1958
Reprinted 1974 with permission of Cambridge University Press
and with an additional prefatory note in an unabridged
edition as an Archon Book, an imprint of
The Shoe String Press, Inc.
Hamden, Connecticut 06514

Printed in the United States of America

To

JACQUES MARITAIN

Whose affection and admiration
for my country are equalled
by mine for his

CONTENTS

Preface   *page* ix

 I Movements of the Mind, *c.* 1570–*c.* 1660
    1. Towards quantitative precision   6
    2. Towards modern science   17

 II The Genesis of Industrialism
    1. The Renaissance and industrial growth   36
    2. The Reformation and the weakening of despotism,
       c. 1540–*c.* 1640   43
    3. Towards a quantitative economy   50
    4. Towards modern technology   54
    5. Towards the reinforcement of technology by science   62

 III The Origin of Civilization
    1. The limits of natural science   65
    2. Limitations on violence before modern times   68

 IV The Spiritual Basis of Civilization
    1. The waning of medieval reality   83
    2. The Reformation and religious asceticism   87
    3. The infusion of charity into modern reality   91

 V The Aesthetic Basis of Civilization
    1. The Renaissance cult of delight   107
    2. Towards an ethical content   109
    3. Towards greater clarity   123

 VI Civilization and Industrialism
    1. A new economy of delight   128
    2. The 'peaceful conversion' of Chablais   139
    3. The *salon*   145
    4. Quality and industrial civilization   149

Index   157

PREFACE

According to the generous terms of the Wiles Trust, it is possible for the lecturer to offer the public historical work in progress. That is the principal excuse for the appearance of this book. It follows at rather more than a year's distance the first set of Wiles Lectures, Professor Butterfield's *Man on His Past*.

Ever since I began my historical researches thirty-five years ago, I have been concerned with the origins of the industrialized world in which we find ourselves. Under the influence of the view which then prevailed in university circles (and which prevails perhaps even more now), that all serious historical work has to be specialized, I sought these origins, as many others have done, in the field of economic history. I sought them in what was in one way a very narrow branch of that field—the rise of the British coal industry. As time went on, I came to realize that, not only my own effort as a specialist, but the whole approach to the problem of origins in terms of economic history was a partial approach. More recently, especially in the process of writing this book, following the lectures which were delivered at The Queen's University of Belfast in May, I came to realize something which is perhaps even more important. A knowledge of general history is bound to change man's outlook on economic history, and in all probability on the other separate channels into which specialized research has divided the study of history during the past hundred years or so. Economic history, as presented not only by historian specialists, such as the elder Arnold Toynbee (who first set forth systematically the idea of an 'industrial revolution'), but by Karl Marx (who is considered to be an historical philosopher, a philosopher and even the founder of a gospel), is not only incomplete as an explanation of industrial civilization; it is unsatisfactory even as a partial explanation. The subject needs to be thought through anew in terms of man's experience as a whole, if it is to be presented to the public in all countries in ways that could be of greater service to a true understanding of world history.

Perhaps I should say a word about my equipment for reconsidering economic history and the rise of industrialism from the vantage point of general history. At the outset of my own special researches, my interests and those of my late wife, who was a gifted writer, led me to spend as much time as possible with the great works of literature, music and the visual arts. A little later I was drawn to the study of philosophy and theology, as well as to the general histories of such masters as Herodotus, Tacitus and Gibbon. These subjects commanded an increasing part of my time. They elicited an increasing share of my enthusiasm.

I found myself wondering whether there might be some relation between the faith, the ethics, the art which have been vital to many human beings, and the special subjects of economic inquiry. These subjects would have become lifeless for me if I had looked at them only in terms of the statistics and categories which were offered as almost the whole of wisdom by some economists. Subjects of economic inquiry took on life for me only in terms of the men and women who forced their way to the surface in the documents which I read and of those I met in the process of examining and discussing documents: archivists as well as historians and other learned men who had been trained in their youth in general culture. Most of these contemporaries were specialists, but they had never quite forgotten what they had learned, in spite of the routine and mechanical nature of much of the work they were expected to do, and they also drew on the experience of the lives they led, which inevitably transcended their specialties.

I eventually came to the conclusion that the origin of the unique industrial civilization which involves us all cannot properly be made the special preserve of economic historians.

Preface

I came to the conclusion that the only way this origin might possibly be understood is through the study of history as a whole. I was thus confronted with the task of trying to learn about all channels of history at a time when it was widely accepted as an axiom of scholarship that the only way to know anything serious about one channel was to devote to it a lifetime of research.

This placed me in a dilemma. I saw that it was necessary to go beyond the beaten paths of historical specialization, but that this involved the risk of becoming superficial in one's knowledge of the past. And then, as if that dilemma were not sufficient to complicate one poor life, I found pressing down upon me the conviction that the problem of the origin of industrial civilization is actually an aspect of the problem of its present condition and its future. I became more and more convinced that its future depends on us—on human beings with free will. That we could make industrialism into something enduring for the souls of men only as a result of a free search for truth in every line of inquiry, philosophical and theological and artistic, as well as historical. I do not mean a search for truth in the specific sense in which the natural scientist or the social scientist is committed to seek for it. The truth that seems necessary is one which aims to comprehend every facet of man's existence. That is just the truth which the modern insistence on specialization and classification virtually forbids us to seek, or at any rate fails to provide us with any established media through which to seek it.

The future of history, the future of knowledge, and the future of civilization itself, are thus interdependent. If we are to examine the nature of this interdependence, the use of methods derived from nineteenth-century natural science are most inadequate.

I can hardly hope to have made more than a beginning in my attempt to solve these two dilemmas. But they have to be stated and they have to be faced. That is what I tried to do in my lectures in Belfast. In the light of the discussions that

Preface

followed each lecture, and in the light of the sober and difficult meditations of a European summer, I have tried again in this book. I have become increasingly certain that, in spite of the risks, the only way to handle this subject of the cultural foundations of industrial civilization is to seek for the universal in the particulars of many fields of historical inquiry, and to do this, so far as my inadequate equipment and talent allow, without losing sight of the fact that the triumph of industrialism has raised in an acute form the problem of the survival of the human spirit in the temporal world. The chapters that follow suggest that it was mainly the human spirit that created industrialism as we find it. They suggest further that in the long run the only way men might meet and surmount the threat of destruction which confronts them today and which will not disappear tomorrow is through the renewal and the perfection of that spirit to which men and women owe their greatness.

I am sure I am not entirely wrong in thinking that it was a sense of this power of the human spirit, and of the way in which history as studied and taught sometimes gets in the way of its improvement, which led Mrs Austen T. Boyd, in her wise generosity, to found the Wiles Trust. Sir Eric Ashby, the Master of Peterhouse and Professor Michael Roberts, who had charge of the arrangements of the lectures and discussions, have given the lectureship the sound basis of serious inquiry and careful scholarship on which it rests. I know of no lectureship which equals this one in the opportunities it offers an historian to transcend specialties, to set forth ideas and to discuss them at length with his professional peers. Through partially successful attempts to reconcile scholarly criticism with work of interest to the general public will depend the influence of the Wiles Trust upon the historical outlook of the generations to come—a matter of much moment to the founder.

The invitation to deliver the second series of these lectures and to publish them was one which I could not refuse in view of the development of my own interests. But I accepted with much hesitation, and I publish this historical essay with trepidation, because of the vastness of the undertaking and my continual sense of my own inadequate preparation. In the past fifteen years I have made several efforts to meet the mission to which, for want of a more adequate candidate, I seem to have been summoned. This effort in connexion with the Wiles Trust has interested me at least as much as any of the others. But, knowing a little how far short it falls of what it should be and could be, I can only hope that it will not be my last effort, and that readers and critics will be indulgent because of its provisional nature.

As it happened, the invitation to deliver the Wiles Lectures came shortly after I had received a grant from the Rockefeller Foundation for research in connexion with a long work on the same subject. This financial support has been indispensable in preparing the present book, which is to be regarded as an attempt to break the ground for what I hope will be a more comprehensive history, going more deeply into the origins of industrial civilization, taking account of the influence upon it of the Near and Far East, and bringing the story of its rise and triumph down to the present.

To the members of the Wiles Trust, to Sir Eric and Lady Ashby and to Mr and Mrs Boyd in particular, I owe an immense debt of gratitude for their hospitality and kindness in Belfast and afterwards. And I am under great obligations to Professor Roberts and to the group of scholars who gave the time and made the effort to come to Belfast and to participate in the discussion, some of them old friends of mine: Professor Butterfield (who is now so closely linked to The Queen's University through the Wiles Trust), Professor Cobban, Professor Briggs, Dr Hugh Trevor-Roper, Dr H. G. Koenigsberger, Dr A. R. Hall, Dr T. Halliman and Mr E. Kerridge. These discussions, which are a special feature of this lectureship, are of the greatest value to the lecturer. Their value is increased by the participation of members of the Department of History, as well as of some members from the Departments of Philosophy, Spanish, French, German, English and Economics, in The Queen's University of Belfast.

Outside Belfast, two friends—one old and one new—have come to my assistance this summer in reading the manuscript of this book with a generosity and a serious purpose which have helped me greatly and for which I am profoundly grateful. Mr André Siegfried, of the French Academy, has lent his moral support and his critical faculties to the undertaking as a whole. Mrs Russell Davenport has saved me from several serious errors in judgement. She has helped me in putting the subject of economic history in its proper perspective in relation to the more important matters treated in the book.

I am also grateful to Miss Nellie Kerling and to Mademoiselle Robinet for their invaluable help with material available in the English and French archives, and to Mademoiselle Georgette Houdebine for putting the final touches on the typescript here in Paris. My major obligation both for research and typing is to my secretary, Mrs R. Armour. Her accuracy, speed and initiative are beyond praise. I could never have got the book ready to meet the deadline which the end of summer represented without her continuous help during the past two years in Chicago.

The provisional character of this small book seems to forbid an attempt to supply elaborate references in the footnotes. Among the references given there is, I realize, disproportionately frequent mention of my own books and articles. My reasons for including so many of these citations are two. First, these lectures have grown largely out of material that has appeared in essays that I have published during the past twenty-five years. Consequently there seems no point in repeating here sources that are available already in footnotes printed as part of those essays. Secondly, it has occurred to me that an occasional reader of this present book might possibly wish to examine parts of the text of earlier scholarly efforts of mine, and that unless I cite chapter and verse he will have

Preface

great difficulty in finding these, as my essays have appeared in widely scattered places and under varied auspices, some in England, some in the United States, some in France and in French, and one only in Italian, which alas *I* neither speak nor readily understand!

JOHN NEF

PARIS
28 September 1956

Prefatory Note

Since the nineteen-thirties I have concerned myself with a new kind of historical writing. It revolves not around political events, as did the general histories written prior to the nineteenth century, but around the interrelations between developments in various fields of human endeavor, about which the special inquiries of the past hundred and fifty years have revealed so much unknown before. While my concern has been mainly with Europe, and particularly with Great Britain and France during the two centuries preceding the Industrial Revolution, I have recognized the importance of comparisons with America, Asia and other parts of the world.

My principal historical works form a corpus. *Cultural Foundations of Industrial Civilization*, first published in 1958 (emanating from the Wiles Lectures delivered in 1956 at the Queen's University in Belfast), is an essential part of the story I am trying to tell. My effort to understand the historical factors behind the adoption of heat energy as the source of mechanical power began with a consideration of the role of price changes in generating, especially in England during the Elizabethan

XV

and Stuart periods, a kind of preliminary economic revolution in agriculture and in industry. That inquiry into price changes was followed by a study of the part played by the English seventeenth century political revolutions in orienting enterprise in the direction of the Industrial Revolution at the end of the eighteenth century and after. I then undertook a more comprehensive study of the respective roles of war and peace in the coming of the unique mechanized world we now know. Subsequent studies dealt with the parts played by religious institutions and by scientific thought in the age of the scientific revolution.

Thus an attempt has been made to draw together what the late Crane Brinton referred to as "economic history" and "intellectual history", a combination which, as he put it, "results . . . in an enrichment of history pure and simple." A book published in French (and translated into Japanese and Italian) aimed to sketch the interrelations between these and divers other historical factors. It is called *La Naissance de la civilisation industrielle et le monde contemporain*, Paris (Colin) 1954. The Wiles Lectures dealt with various cultural factors neglected in this and in earlier studies of mine.

Since 1958 some of these studies have been revised and made more explicit in *The Conquest of the Material World*, Chicago, 1964. The meaning of the whole corpus is considered in a book to be published in 1973 by Public Affairs Press in Washington entitled *Search for Meaning*.

JOHN NEF

1973

I

MOVEMENTS OF THE MIND

c. 1570–c. 1660

The distinguished French writer, Georges Bernanos, was on the island of Majorca during the early phases of the recent Spanish Civil War. He was profoundly shocked by what he saw: by the liquidation without trial of men and women who were suspected of sympathizing with the cause of the Spanish Republic. The shock suggested the title—*Les grands cimetières sous la lune*—of his book of protest against the disintegration of decent standards of judgement and of conduct that he felt was taking place among the Christian peoples, particularly those of western Europe. When he visited General Franco's headquarters, he is said to have expressed his disgust to some of the leading officers. He spoke to them of the *barbarism* with which cemeteries were being dug to bury the mutilated bodies of the victims taken from their homes and shot in the night. One of these officers replied that Frenchmen are only lukewarm in their Christian faith. They suppose the supreme virtue is to die for Christ when in fact it is to kill for Him![1]

This incident reminds us that violence, bloody death and death by incineration are part of Christian history. It introduces us to that age whose part in forming the cultural foundations for industrial civilization it is our purpose to examine. Fighting and killing in the name of Christ were probably never so common within Europe as during the last half of the sixteenth century. In the reigns of Elizabeth I of England and Philip II of Spain, differences over religious

[1]Subsequent to the publication of this book, M. Maritain, whom my memory used as my authority for this episode, pointed out to me that as far as he knew Bernanos never visited the headquarters of General Franco and that this remark of a Spanish officer was often mentioned in France at the time but not as having been said directly to Bernanos.

issues became one of the major causes for war between states, between factions inside states, and even between members of the same family. The kind of slaughter against which Bernanos protested was almost endemic to many parts of Europe.

We think of Montaigne rightly as one of the most humane men of those times. A letter that he wrote on 24 August 1562, at the beginning of the long era of so-called religious wars which was to last for nearly a century, suggests that he, like Bernanos four hundred years afterwards, was sorrowful over the spectacle of violent and cruel human nature engaged in civil strife. But his words suggest also a resignation, which permeates his *Essays* and which separates him from Bernanos. He does not attribute the callous ways in which men are committing and accepting murder and rape to any decadence in standards of conduct or to any weakening of the human conscience. Writing to a royal official in Paris, he said:

I have already put you in possession, Monsieur, of the troubles which desolated the Agenois and Périgord, where our common friend, Mesney, taken prisoner, was brought to Bordeaux and had his head cut off. I wish to tell you now that those of Nérac, having by the indiscretion of the young captain of this town, lost from a hundred to a hundred and twenty men in a skirmish against a troop of Montluc, withdrew into Béarn with their ministers, not without great danger of their lives, about the fifteenth day of July, at which time those of Castel Jalous surrendered, of which place the minister was executed. Those of Marmande, Saint Macaire, and Bazas fled likewise, but not without a cruel loss, for immediately the château of Duras was pillaged, and that of Monseigneur Villette was forced, where there were two citizens and a large number of churchmen. There every cruelty and violence were exercised, the first day of August, without regard to quality, sex, or age. Montluc violated the daughter of the minister, who was slain with the others. I am extremely sorry to tell you that in this massacre were involved our kinswoman, the wife of Gaspard Duprat, and two of her children; it was a noble woman, whom I have had opportunities of often seeing when I went into those parts, and at whose house I was always assured of enjoying good hospitality. In short, I say no more

to you at present, for the recital causes me severe pain, and therefore
I pray God to have you in His holy keeping....[1]

Montaigne was living in a period of strain and fear, not
unlike our own, with Europe on the brink of total war. It is
therefore something more than mere curiosity which leads a
historian to consider what men's minds and imaginations
were able to do for the later welfare of the human race during
the critical times which lasted from the mid-sixteenth to the
mid-seventeenth century, from the abdication of Charles V
and the accession of Elizabeth I to the Peace of the Pyrenees
and the Restoration. Let us try to clarify a little what were
the basic changes in human thought, in faith, in art and in
conduct during this age, and how these changes were associated with the eventual coming of industrial civilization. If
we raise the question how these changes took place, how far
they resulted from the exercise of man's free will in a Europe
frequently at war, we can perhaps help our contemporaries
and our descendants to recognize the forces in human nature
which need to be encouraged as a means of meeting the dangers
that beset men and women everywhere today, and especially
those that confront the chief nations of the earth, armed as
they now are with weapons so powerful that they would be
safe only in the hands of God the Father.

Historical inquiries concerning the origins of industrialism
have been preoccupied for the past two generations with
Marxian notions of progress, and with the part played by
technical changes in methods of production, transportation,
communication and administration in bringing into being
the mechanized world in which we live. This preoccupation
has led students and scholars to centre their attention upon
changes in economic conditions, in seeking for the causes for
the coming of industrial civilization, whether in the immediate
or the more distant past. In this search the place of the

[1] *Essays of Montaigne*, translated by Charles Cotton, I (ed. W. C. Hazlitt; London,
1902), xliii–iv.

human personality has been largely limited to those ideas, to those intellectual discoveries, which can be seen as factors contributing to utility, as that word is widely understood: to the abridgement of human labour, the multiplication of output, to reductions in the cost and increases in the speed of transport and communication, to the prolongation of the average span of human life by the conquest of disease. It is often forgotten that the concept of utility that prevails in our time is largely the result of economic speculations, of the practical applications of scientific knowledge and of a concentration upon certain kinds of inventions, especially those which substitute machinery for manual labour. The utility of faith, of workmanship, of beauty, of everything that nourishes the soul and that is beyond price, has been forgotten or denied.

Has not this preoccupation with particular aspects of the influence of human genius produced a one-sided view of the genesis of the contemporary industrialized world? Did not the development of both faith and art also help to create the civilization of the eighteenth and early nineteenth centuries in Europe and America?

Before we can consider the place of faith, of moral values and of art in the world that we have inherited, we have to consider the consequences of the gradual separation of both from scientifically accepted knowledge. In so far as the conditions of the contemporary world have been achieved by the works of the mind and the efforts of the will, the *direct* causes of the great wealth and the vast population can hardly be found in the inventions of faith and the inventions of art.

The very separation of science from faith, from ethics and from art, which is so characteristic of our times, is at the roots of the industrialized world in which we live. In a letter destined for Fermat, which he sent to Father Mersenne in 1637, Descartes remarked that the great Toulouse mathematician seemed to suppose 'that in saying a thing is easy to believe, I meant only to say that it is probable. This is far

4

from my position: I consider everything that is only probable as almost false....'[1] Such a position has led to the admission as true of only what is verifiable in tangible and increasingly in measurable terms, or in terms of mathematical demonstrations which start from propositions artificially divorced from the actual experience of living. Since it is impossible, as Pascal seems to have been the first to recognize, to offer the same kind of tangible proof and to get the same kind of assent in matters of faith, of morals and of beauty, the truths of religion, moral philosophy and art have come to be treated as subjects of private opinion rather than of public knowledge. Their contributions to the contemporary world are *indirect*, though not for that reason necessarily inferior to those of science.

A revolution in the ways human minds work seems to manifest itself differently from a revolution in the economic life of human societies. Startlingly rapid industrial changes—startlingly rapid changes in the ways men exploit the earth, produce and transport commodities and transmit messages—such changes are revolutionary, one may say, only if they affect a large proportion of the population, and alter radically their habits of work, of transportation, of consumption and of communication. The revolutionary stage in intellectual history is, on the contrary, generally the stage in which a few powerful minds emphasize certain hitherto neglected values and methods, and relate them potentially in novel ways to the life of action which individuals and societies have to lead in order to inhabit the earth. Innovations are usually brought about by the exceptionally powerful thinkers, the exceptionally inspired hearts, the exceptionally fertile and disciplined imaginations. Up to the present, the life of the mind, in the sense of that inner spiritual life that affects history, has never been the life of masses of men and women. It has influenced directly those who have been able to participate in the works of the few by reading, enacting or contemplating them. What

[1] *Œuvres de Fermat*, eds. Paul Tannery and Charles Henry, II (Paris, 1894), 113.

has made new ideas influential has been the fact that considerable numbers of persons have shared in these ways the experiences of the most seminal minds, the exaltation of the most saintly characters, or the delight of the greatest artists.

These innovations that have affected history are probably not unrelated to the thought and to the work of a much larger number of men and women. It would seem that there should be at least a twofold relationship. The innovators derive their ideas not only from solitary reflexion, but in no small measure from their experiences with others, and some of these others, who influence the masters, have experiences of their own which are reflected in the works of the masters. Again, in certain kinds of creative labour, for instance in the founding of a religious order or in the construction and embellishment of a building, such as a cathedral, a church, a town hall or a château, results depend not only on one or a few leaders, but on considerable numbers of associates and followers who conceive and create in the same spirit, but with a large measure of personal initiative.

I. TOWARDS QUANTITATIVE PRECISION

Today, whether we are concerned with the public, with the administrator, with the business executive, the manager and engineer, or with the learned man, we are struck by the place most people give, almost instinctively, to quantitative statements as a basis for judging their own welfare and that of the groups, societies and nations to which they belong. If the price of shares is rising, if the production of commodities is increasing in volume, if profits and wages are higher than they ever were before, if the labour costs of mining and manufacturing are falling, almost every one who reads about these matters in the daily or weekly papers feels at least momentarily better. If he reads that there has been a fall in these barometers of public health, his spirits are depressed. In the modern world hundreds of thousands, even millions, of people are employed to gather, classify and present in a readily understandable form myriads of statistics. This is the result of a growing thirst for quantitative information that began generations ago, and that has recently been increased artificially by the new means of communication, especially by the hurried journalism which, in its search for speed and for short cuts, finds statistical information, provided by numerous accounting firms and bureaux (public and private), the easiest material to consult, because its use requires usually very little thought.

One of my most industrious colleagues, who had spent more than a decade on an historical work of remarkable erudition, sent a copy to a relative of his, a chemical engineer. He showed me the letter of praise which he later received. The engineer went to work and added up all the references in the three huge volumes. He discovered that they ran into five figures. Therefore he concluded the work must be important. Less time, and especially less effort, was required to make this addition than to read the book, and anyway by what criteria could the book of a specialist be judged if it were read by a specialist in another subject?

Like a book, a man is now judged, publicly at any rate, not by his character or the quality of his work, but by the salary he is paid or the total income he receives. Numerical figures occupy a place in the modern vocabulary of values that they have never occupied before.

People's minds have not always worked in that way. When did they begin to do so? And what, in the beginning, had the new emphasis on quantitative values to do with the separation of natural science from faith and art, which enabled scientists to focus their attention on tangible problems, and helped to bring about eventually an unprecedented alliance between scientific knowledge and material progress?

In his recent book, *Le Problème de l'incroyance au 16ème siècle ou La Religion de Rabelais*, Lucien Febvre has suggested

7

that the Europeans of Rabelais' times, compared with their descendants today, were little interested in their exact age. It was by no means as universal then as it has since become for people to remember just how old they were, if indeed they had ever known. Rabelais himself perhaps knew less about his age than his modern biographers profess to know, though they disagree among themselves as to the date of his birth. 'People generally, in Rabelais' times,' Febvre wrote, 'do not seem to have felt an imperious need for precision.'[1]

During the hundred years that followed Rabelais' death in 1553, there are many indications that exact time, exact quantities, exact distances were coming to have a greatly increased interest for men and women in connexion with private and public life. One of the most impressive examples of the new concern with precision was the action taken by the Church of Rome to provide a more exact calendar. Throughout the Middle Ages the ways in which the Christian peoples measured the passage of time were based on calculations made before the fall of the Roman Empire. The Julian calendar of A.D. 325 was still in use in the age of Rabelais.

Here we have one of many examples of the ways in which the practical sides of European life at the beginning of the sixteenth century were still based on thinking done in other societies, without any fundamental innovations. The Julian calendar made the year too long by 11 minutes and 14 seconds. Seven or eight days were gained every thousand years. For many generations before the Reformation, certainly as far back as the eighth century, learned men, perhaps first among them the venerable Bede, had realized that the calendar they had inherited would eventually no longer coincide with the seasons of the year.

Projects for a new calendar had been considered before the second half of the sixteenth century. But the actual reconstruction took place during the papacy of Gregory XIII, in the decade of the Spanish Armada. It took place in the midst

---

[1] *Le Problème de l'incroyance*, pp. 158, 429.

of the religious civil wars in France and the Low Countries. It was in March 1582 that the Pope issued the brief abolishing the ancient Julian calendar.

Six months later the year was straightened out and brought almost into focus with the exact passage of time, by dropping out ten days and reckoning the day following the feast of St Francis, 5 October, as 15 October. This was done simultaneously in Spain and Portugal, as well as in Rome and other parts of Italy. In France the ten days were suppressed in December; in the Catholic states of Germany in the following year, 1583.

The Gregorian calendar is not the greatest experiment in accuracy of its kind, for the Mayan calendar was apparently more precise. But the Europeans in the late sixteenth century were only on the threshold of those enormous advances in precision which today have subjected human life to a control by exact calculations such as no societies of the past ever experienced. As a symptom of the growing efforts at accuracy which have done so much to transform the rhythm of life and the habits of human beings in more recent times, the Gregorian calendar is enormously impressive. It was about three hundred times as accurate as the calendar which it replaced. The Gregorian calendar is sufficiently accurate to satisfy us today when our standards of accuracy in general have become much more exacting. Twenty thousand years hence, if any of our species are still alive, our descendants should be less than a day out; if we had stuck to the old system of reckoning they would be finding themselves in winter when the calendar registered summer. The change effected in methods of calculating the passage of time in the late sixteenth century was sufficient to relieve us from bothering about this matter of measurement. The societies that are competing for dominion in the twentieth century can hardly hope to survive unless a world civilization based on Christ and the example He set us is achieved. If it is not achieved, there will be no need for calendars. If it is achieved, the

Gregorian calendar will be good enough for a very much longer time to come than seems to concern any practical man today.

Is not this prodigious advance in accuracy indicative of an immense intellectual and administrative effort? Do not things of this kind get done because a growing number of persons feel the desire to do them intensely enough so that a few go about actively getting them done? While the need for a reform of the calendar grew increasingly obvious with the passage of the generations, that seems insufficient to explain why the decisive correction of this wide error in calculation should have occurred in the last quarter of the sixteenth century, rather than fifty or a hundred years earlier or later. Is it not reasonable to suppose that a novel concern arose at this particular time over getting the length of the year straightened out?

The history of the calendar suggests that a greater emphasis then began to be laid on quantitative accuracy than ever before. The quantitative-mindedness that was destined to become a characteristic and distinguishing feature of the contemporary world was so accentuated that Europe came to occupy for the first time a place apart from both the Near and the Far East. Europe began to give a greater importance to the quantitative sides of human experience and speculation than any great societies of the past.

The Europeans were striving after a higher degree of quantitative accuracy in many domains during the span of the eighty years or so that followed. Some of them attached a novel importance to the amassing of statistics, and notably of statistics concerning rates of increase, as guides to economic policy, at the very period when, with Bodin, Malynes, Laffemas, Montchrétien and Mun, economics first emerged as a separate subject of human speculative inquiry, independent both of housekeeping, the concern of each of us in his daily active life, and of moral philosophy, the concern of us all for the guidance of our inner lives.

Towards quantitative precision

Thirty years ago I stumbled on an example of what now seems to me to be a changing attitude concerning the uses to which the statistical information, that had been available for centuries, might fruitfully be put. Neophyte that I was in the subject of history (and particularly in the view of history that the Wiles Trust is now encouraging me to put forward for examination), I had at the time no idea of the possible historical significance of my discovery.

As many historical researchers know, old records have been preserved of the quantities of goods shipped to and from almost every English port, coastwise as well as overseas. Most of the documents are in the Public Record Office in London. There is a notable increase in the materials available during the times of the first Queen Elizabeth, whose reign began in 1558. This is partly an accident of preservation. But it is also the result of a new system of keeping accounts that was then introduced. Hitherto the particulars of ships' cargoes, outward and inward, as recorded by the customs officers of a port, had been usually entered, not in books, but on rolls. Henceforth they were entered habitually in books.

As a young man, working on the early history of the British coal industry, I came on these port books and on the previous rolls. I saw that they might provide a statistical picture of the growth in the coal trade. What I sought, not unnaturally in view of the quantitative-mindedness of the age in which we live, was a statistical picture, year by year, of the increase in the shipments of coal from about 1550 to 1700. Many hundreds of the port books containing entries of coal during those 150 years are still available. I set myself the task of digging out all of these entries, according to the principles of exhaustive research that were then coming to be regarded as the mark of a good historian.

This, I soon found, would require months, if not years. The customs officials, who kept the books, had simply recorded the shipments on which they had collected duties, as had been the practice of tax collectors in Europe for generations, at least from the beginning of the fourteenth century. The laboriousness of my work was increased because the cargoes of each ship were listed together, and coal was mixed in with many other kinds of commodities—for example, with glass, salt, iron, alum and cloth (which was entered under a variety of different names intelligible only to experts on the history of the textile industry). The use of ink in the Record Office is forbidden! Every day during the hours when it was then open, from 10.0 a.m. to 4.30 p.m., I laboriously extracted with my pencil, one by one, the items of coal in each ship. I then took home my working sheets for each port book and added them up in the late afternoons and evenings amid the charms of domestic life.

In those days the hoofs of time seemed to thunder less loudly at my back than they do now, and so I found considerable pleasure in this slow work. Nevertheless, I remember wishing, not infrequently, that the process of extraction could be speeded up.

On one occasion I had a windfall. I came on a small piece of paper, carefully preserved among the bulky rolls and books which form the staple of the customs records. To my astonishment, on this paper were scrawled in the late Elizabethan handwriting the total shipments of coal year by year for seven years, from Michaelmas 1591 through Michaelmas 1598, from Newcastle upon Tyne, then the greatest centre of the coal trade in the world. I had in my hands, ready-made, a statistical table of just the kind I had been seeking in vain, a table which made it possible to determine the rate of increase in coal shipments from the Tyne for this uninterrupted series of years. I could not have worked out the table myself because nearly all the port books for those years are now missing from the Record Office.

Why was such a reckoning made? Who was my unknown benefactor?

At the end of the year 1598 Lord Buckhurst was on the point of succeeding Lord Burghley in the great office of

Lord Treasurer. On 6 December he wrote to a man named Fanshaw, apparently one of the principal customs officials:

> To my loving friend Mr Fanshaw or to his deputy or chief clark. Mr Fanshaw I am for her Majesty's services to require you to make a collection for 7 years past. How many caldron of coal have been carried out of England to any port beyond the seas as likewise how much has been brought to London or to any other port in England from New Castle. I mean for all from Newcastle. I pray you do it in all speed and deliver it to Richard Couch and his bearer.

Fanshaw and his staff apparently spent some two weeks doing for Buckhurst the kind of work I was later to do for myself. But the first statistics they supplied were of little value either to Buckhurst's purpose or mine. They gave global figures for the entire seven-year period: 95,558 chaldrons shipped overseas, 418,201 chaldrons shipped coastwise. Buckhurst expressed his annoyance in a curt note written on 21 December:

> Mr Fanshaw this is a certificat of confusion more tending to blind than to inform...I require you to set downe every of the said seven yeares in particular, according to the request of my note unto you.[1]

Fanshaw and his staff complied with Buckhurst's request and broke down the figures year by year. But while doing so one of them noted, as if to suggest how unreasonable their master was showing himself to be, '13651 is the 7 part of the coles transported [overseas]'. Buckhurst could have worked out the *average* for himself in a few minutes. This comment suggests that the distinction between the average traffic and the *rate of increase* was still meaningless to these customs officers. But the distinction was obviously clear to Buckhurst. The force with which he insisted on getting the figures that he wanted suggests that it was as vital a distinction for him at the end of the sixteenth century as it is for us in the mid-twentieth.

[1] P.R.O. Exch. K.R. Customs Accounts, 111/40.

Movements of the Mind

The problem of finding money to balance the state's budget is perennial. During the last years of Elizabeth's reign, among other expedients, one for raising new revenue from the coal trade was under discussion. Doubtless the treasury officials at Westminster in 1598 were aware, as I had become aware in 1923 before I turned to the port books for proof, that coal was a growing traffic towards the end of the sixteenth century. What was unusual was that Buckhurst wanted to know, as anyone in his position today would know as a matter of routine, precisely how rapidly it was growing. Presumably he wanted to project the rates of increase into the future as a means of estimating roughly the revenue which might eventually be obtained from the taxes that he was about to levy on both the coastwise and the overseas traffic in coal.

Medieval Europeans had been able to count. Double-entry book-keeping went back at least to the early fourteenth century.[1] During the fourteenth and fifteenth centuries tax collectors in assessing poll taxes, other tax collectors in levying imposts and tolls at sea ports and along the great rivers or at metallurgical works, had counted the number of hearths in a town, the quantity of various kinds of cloth shipped, the amount of silver extracted from argentiferous lead ores. Some of this data is still preserved in archives. The modern student of history, with his interest in exact quantities, can use them to estimate the size of the population of such places as Toulouse or Paris, the volume of cloth shipped from Rouen or London, the output of silver in the Tirol. It is possible to work out, as Professor Mollat has done, the growth in the traffic in some commodities for the principal ports of Normandy during the fifteenth and early sixteenth centuries.

---

[1] But it has been suggested that the idea of applying the system of double-entry book-keeping to the finances of the state was a novelty at the end of the sixteenth century. It was at that time that the Dutch mathematician and fortress builder, Simon Stevin, called the attention of Sully to this possibility (Michel Steichen, *Mémoire sur la Vie et les Travaux de Simon Stevin*, Brussels, 1846, p. 98). For the spread, in previous years, of the technique of double-entry book-keeping in Europe, see Raymond de Roover, *Jan Ympyn, Essai historique et technique sur le premier traité flamand de comptabilité* (1543), pp. 5–6 *et passim*.

Towards quantitative precision

This knowledge, which has cost an immense amount of historical research, is in a sense quite unhistorical. Medieval Europeans were unaware of the statistical facts about their time that the erudite modern medievalist teaches his students. Some of us know more accurately than men of the thirteenth, fourteenth and fifteenth centuries knew themselves, the population of their cities and towns, the output of silver in certain districts, the volume of trade for certain ports. We think of our European ancestors before the mid-sixteenth century in ways that would have seemed strange to them, and some of us write their history in terms they would not have understood. The experts employed by Hollywood motion picture producers who years ago put in the mouth of Henry VIII (in a film version of Shakespeare's play) the words: 'my little kingdom of three million inhabitants', were on reasonably firm statistical ground. But how could Henry VIII have been aware of figures concerning population which have been derived from old records only during the past hundred years? And even if he had had an inkling of the number of persons in the kingdom, he was hardly quantitative-minded enough to express himself like a modern Chancellor of the Exchequer.

Students of economic history, seeking the origins of statistics as a learned discipline, are now inclined to trace the beginnings of the subject back as far as the second half of the seventeenth century. At that time, a number of persons in England, among them Sir William Petty, who was born in 1623, and Gregory King, who was born in 1648, began to compute out of curiosity (and no doubt also because of the contribution that it was coming to be believed the knowledge might make to economic policy) series of figures for periods of years concerning population, trade, the national consumption of food and drink, the national dividend of goods and services. They began to work out rates of growth (*taux d'accroissement*) and to project them into the future. For example, Petty estimated in 1682 that if the population of London and that of England and Wales continued to increase at the rates which he thought prevailed in the seventeenth century, by 1840 practically the entire population of the kingdom, which he predicted would then be 10,917,389, would be living in the city! So he predicted further the growth of the city would stop before 1800 when London would have rather more than five million inhabitants![1] This is not a startling example of prevision, but early twentieth-century statisticians have not done much better with their demographic predictions.

Such examples of idle speculative philosophy in the service of quantitative data became striking for the first time after the English Restoration. But do not their origins reach farther back? Do not the eighty years or so preceding the Restoration constitute a period when a few men committed themselves to statistical inquiries concerning rates of increase to a degree that had hardly ever been reached before? Three years earlier than Buckhurst's inquiry into the exact quantity of coals shipped, Burghley had asked the same Fanshaw to search the customs books of Dover and Sandwich to find out what custom had been paid for the transport of lime during the previous eight or ten years.[2] Have we not, therefore, during the last years of the sixteenth century, the beginnings of that interest in the exact quantitative expansion of trade that has since become characteristic of practical economics?

The late sixteenth century was the time when in Spain figures were printed giving the population of provinces and the population of towns. It was the time when the Italians also began to take a serious interest in population statistics— in the making of censuses. It was the period when in France a controversy was carried on between Bodin and a certain Monsieur de Malestroict concerning the relations of the quantity of money in circulation to the level of prices. While it is probable that earlier precedents can be found for all these inquiries, it is at this time that such inquiries took on the

---

[1] *Another Essay in Political Arithmetick* (London, 1683); in *The Economic Writings of Sir William Petty*, ed. C. H. Hull, II (Cambridge, 1899), 464.
[2] K.R. Customs Accounts, 111/40.

character of a European movement of the mind. Professor Dion, of the Collège de France, tells me that in viticulture this was the first time when proprietors began to plant vineyards primarily for reasons of economy, where natural conditions of the soil and climate made it possible to produce wine most cheaply. When we are searching for the origins of our modern quantitative-mindedness, we are bound to give a special importance to the last decades of the sixteenth century.

2. TOWARDS MODERN SCIENCE

It was soon after the times of Henry VIII and Rabelais, then, that the outlook of a few men on matters of quantity began to change rapidly, and that the scope of quantitative calculations spread to the realm of public policy. The change was accompanied by a novel concern in finding ways of speeding up arithmetical calculations: addition, subtraction, multiplication and division.

It is hard for us to realize how laborious and slow were the means at the disposal of medieval Europeans for dealing with calculations 'which seem to us of the simplest character'.[1] The introduction of Arabic numbers into Europe provided more easily manipulated counters than the Roman numbers, and the use of Arabic numbers seems to have spread rapidly towards the end of the sixteenth century, at least on the Continent. Between about 1590 and 1617 John Napier invented his curious 'bones' for calculating. He followed this invention with his more celebrated discovery of logarithms. This was widely adopted all over Europe almost at once, and in consequence arithmetical calculations were immensely accelerated. This was apparently also the period when the ancient habit of adding and subtracting from left to right, which still prevailed, according to Lucien Febvre, until the end

---

[1] Florence A. Yeldham, *The Story of Reckoning in the Middle Ages* (London, 1926), pp. 30, 46.

of the sixteenth century, began to be superseded by the much quicker way of making them from right to left.[1]

This new passion for precision and for expressing values in figures had a close relation to the most momentous movements of the mind of the age, those in connexion with scientific investigations. Speculative thought relating to physics, astronomy and biology had an established and honourable place in the history of the Greeks and Romans of antiquity. It had not been entirely eclipsed in Europe during the centuries of the barbarian invasions, and it took a new lease on history with the rise of European scholastic philosophy, of Romanesque and Gothic art, from the late eleventh century onwards.

But the views which prevailed (like other views which had prevailed in various parts of the world, such as China and India, where great sophisticated societies had developed) concerning material phenomena, the methods of seeking knowledge of the physical and the biological world, and the problems that the mathematicians sought to solve, were in the main fundamentally different from the views, the methods and the problems that have come to prevail in the realm of scientific and mathematical speculation in modern times. There is now general agreement among historians that the new scientific outlook was brought about by basic changes in the manner, one may almost say in the nature, of speculative thought. What were these changes and when did they occur?

It is difficult to set even an approximate date as the starting point of 'the scientific revolution' which has given men such astonishing new knowledge of space, time, matter and motion. It is conventional to refer to 1500, or to the early sixteenth century, as the beginning. Certainly the discoveries of Copernicus (1473–1543), Fernel (*c.* 1490–1558) and Vesalius (1514–64) point the way to modern science. But it is now rather widely agreed that important distinctions have to be drawn between the most pioneering scientific work of those genera-

---

[1] *Le Problème de l'incroyance*, p. 425.

tions and that of the generations of Galileo (1564–1642), Harvey (1578–1657) and Pascal (1623–62). Such eminent scientists of our times as Sherrington, Schrödinger and Weizsächer are all inclined to separate the scientific work of the period from about 1500 to 1570 sharply from that of the period from about 1570 to 1660. Which was the decisive period in introducing the methods of investigation that proved to be the essential instruments of scientific inquiry ever since?

One of the major distinctions that has to be made between the work of the two periods relates to the place occupied by faith and art in scientific inquiry. It was hardly until the later period that they began to lose their importance as the basis for scientific reasoning.

We must not press this distinction too far or become dogmatic in our views concerning scientific methods. Even today the work of a great scientist still resembles that of an artist, up to the point where palpable proofs become the decisive test. His discoveries are almost always the result of such complicated and subtle developments within the mind itself that the creative process is hardly ever susceptible to explanations, the rational nature of which is self-evident in the same way that the rational nature of scientific proofs becomes self-evident to those who are capable of understanding them.

There is a story about Ruskin and Turner that always touched me. They were in Turner's studio, where Turner had just finished a large canvas. Ruskin was admiring it; he began to explain why it was a great work of art, and he so warmed to his subject (as we professors are also prone to do) that he talked for half an hour without a break. Turner listened attentively; when the lecture was over he smiled with slight indulgence and said simply, 'You know, Ruskin, art's a rum thing!'

Works of genius, in whatever sphere they are produced, are arrived at by complicated and subtle procedures. The artist is rightly dismayed by the critic of art who tells how his mind works when he composes a sonata or writes a poem. He is dismayed still more by the psychologist who explains to him that the creative process is a product of his environment, of his childhood complexes or of his adult disappointments. And even in our times, the great scientist whose original discoveries are the result of intuition may still share some of the artist's distress over attempts to fit his labours into the dreary methodology which is not infrequently superimposed on works of genius by modern scholars and critics.

It is true, nevertheless, that imaginative insight came to occupy a less decisive position as a factor determining scientific results during the period from about 1570 to 1660. Let us take our example from astronomy. It was in 1543 that Copernicus' famous work appeared. In it he argued that the earth is not flat and fixed and the centre of the universe; that it is instead a revolving sphere moving through space, along with a myriad of other spheres. At the same time Vesalius published his influential book on anatomy, while Fernel and Paracelsus were formulating problems of physiology and medicine in ways that seem closer to us than those of any earlier masters. How did their work differ from the scientific work of the generations of Galileo and Descartes?

We think of Copernicus as a supreme innovator concerning the structure of the physical universe, and so he was. But before his time the old notion of the world as flat and immobile was by no means universally held. What he did was to put forward with great authority and force what is still essentially the prevailing view of the motion of the heavenly bodies. But the establishment of his innovation as true demanded a different kind of investigation from his. The new system of the movement of the heavenly bodies, which he felicitously described, was not derived from a 'rational dynamical explanation of these movements'. It was derived from art and theology, from the classical aesthetic concept that 'the most

20

perfect curve...is the circle', and from the religious concept that in God's universe heavenly bodies must move in the most perfect ways. Therefore, Copernicus believed *erroneously* that 'heavenly bodies can move only in perfect circles'.[1]

There are important differences between the final appeal for positive evidence made by Copernicus and his predecessors and the final appeal made by Tycho Brahe (1546–1601) and Kepler (1571–1630). These differences were characteristic of differences between the scientific outlook and methods of the greatest scientific minds of the early sixteenth century and of those whose adult lives began in the fifteen-seventies and eighties. The eye of the artist became especially penetrating, as Professor Butterfield pointed out in his *Origins of Modern Science*, during the times of Copernicus, Fernel and Vesalius. The novel desire, which was then arising, to see nature, including animal and human bodies, as they appear directly to man's senses, was of much help to science.[2] The researches of a few great Renaissance artists, who were almost universal men in the range of their interests and artistic achievements, helped men to see bodies, plants and landscapes afresh in their material reality. But the ways in which the artist and the modern scientist employ sense impressions to create their independent worlds are fundamentally different, and the phenomenal development of science depended partly on a separation of science from art.

What the artists seek above all, when they use their eyes and their other senses, are not precise measurements or exact chemical and physiological behaviour. European artists of the late fifteenth and early sixteenth centuries, some of whom can be perhaps described as artist-scientists, paid greater attention than their predecessors to accurate data. But they were not abandoning the inner vision by means of which the outward

---

[1] C. F. von Weizsäcker, 'The spirit of Natural Science', *Humanitas*, II, no. 1 (1947), 3.
[2] Herbert Butterfield, *The Origins of Modern Science, 1300–1800* (London, 1949), pp. 34–5.

reality which they observed was given permanence in the form of art. Without this inner vision there can be no art. Cézanne is said to have been infuriated by a cartoon which appeared in a newspaper towards the end of his life, when he was beginning to acquire some fame. What struck him as inconceivably false was that the cartoonist represented him with his arms clasped around a tree, saying, 'Oh, if I could only transport this onto my canvas!'

The artist seeks the entire atmosphere surrounding the things observed, and the transfiguration of the essentials into enduring forms such as nature does not provide. His purpose is not to describe natural processes, or even to describe nature, but to incorporate certain materials of nature into art by a process of selection and creation. In the interest of truth and delight the artist seeks not exactly measured quantities, space relationships, or the speed of the movement of bodies through space or of blood through the body—quantities, relationships and movements susceptible to precise empirical verification. The dimensions in metres and centimetres of Chartres Cathedral and the surrounding landscape were not Corot's concern when he did his painting of this scene. The mind that confines itself to statistics and photographs may find the picture false, because Corot has disengaged from the scene traits and a general impression that the photographer and even the architect in his drawings are incapable of conveying. As Marcel Proust once wrote, the verification of a work of art consists in 'la rencontre fortuite avec un grand esprit'.[1] It depends upon the meeting which a serious reader or observer or listener has with a book, a painting or a musical composition—a meeting in which his enthusiasm is enlisted intuitively with abiding enthusiasm (because he recognizes in it something of himself, something he felt dimly before, and something which therefore reveals his own inner life). It depends upon a commitment to what one experiences, not upon any objective proof that can be exactly described and

[1] John Ruskin, *La Bible d'Amiens* (Paris, 1947), Preface by Marcel Proust, p. 92 n.

exactly repeated. The impression conveyed and the material behind it are too subtle, too varied and too comprehensive to be susceptible to such proof. There can be no objective test of the verification; instructed artists sometimes make grievous mistakes in judging the merits of their own works or those of others, mistakes which are less likely to occur when a leading scientist judges the validity of his own work or the work of another scientist. This is because the *natural scientist* usually deals with far more limited categories than the artist, because questions of human nature and destiny hardly enter into his judgements, and because, until very recently, he dealt only with phenomena which could be directly observed and measured.

As long as men looked for scientific knowledge primarily as theologians or as artists, they included in their subject-matter concepts and impressions which are essentially human. As long as they approached their material as theologians or as artists, they were unable to handle it with the peculiar precision and positive accuracy that characterize modern science, and which have dehumanized it. What distinguishes modern science from all science of the past is not the direct examination of nature or of animal and human bodies. It is the rigour with which the scientists have confined themselves in their inquiries, at least until very recently, to the objective analysis and examination of matter, space, time and motion. It is the single-minded application to these inquiries of methods of analysis, known to speculative thinkers before modern times, but cultivated with an intensity in modern times for which there is no historical precedent. The price of such application (for everything we get in life has to be paid for, though not as is too often imagined, in pounds, shillings and pence) was a divorce of the subject-matter and the methods of science from those of art; a divorce which had hardly begun to take place in the mid-sixteenth century.

It may therefore be questioned whether the scientific lessons derived from the early sixteenth century, with the help of an outlook and of methods that served the artist and the man of faith, were actually providing the foundations upon which the modern structure of scientific knowledge has been reared. We should not forget that the fifteenth and early sixteenth centuries in Europe by no means offer the first historical example of sophisticated men looking at nature directly with more piercing eyes than their ancestors of immediately preceding generations. An effort to present a vision of living things, of human bodies in particular, as they really appear to our senses, was no new thing at that time. The twelfth- and thirteenth-century stone images of animals and human beings which we find on Chartres Cathedral and many buildings of the age suggest that medieval artists looked at nature almost as realistically as Renaissance artists. Attic art (as we can see without going to Greece in the statues from the Parthenon brought by Lord Elgin and now in the British Museum) presented the human body with a clarity, perfection, an inevitability, as well as a splendour, which have never been excelled. The great Greek and medieval sculptors were artists, not surgeons or professors of anatomy. Even Hippocrates, the father of medicine, seems to speak as an artist-observer in his descriptions of the behaviour of the body in various diseases, and these descriptions are still in some ways superior to those given by any modern writer. It is debatable whether Vesalius understood the bodily structure of a man better than did the ancient Greeks. He seems, moreover, to have examined his subjects as an artist does, although it is common to refer to him as the father of modern surgery.

The ancients speculated concerning the basic structure of matter and one of the great early Greek philosophers, Democritus, had evolved an atomistic theory not unlike that which is now regarded as true. His theory was vitiated in modern eyes by his attempt to extend the atomistic structure to include the soul, and he may therefore be regarded as one of the earliest materialists. The failure to distinguish what is scientifically subject to analysis from what is not, which

Democritus' confusion concerning the nature of the soul reveals, had not disappeared in the early sixteenth century. (It has not disappeared today, but the greatest scientific thinkers, such as Sherrington, are now clear about the distinction, and take account of it, as their early sixteenth-century predecessors did not.) We have no evidence that in the period of Copernicus, Fernel and Vesalius, any European had as accurate an idea of the structure of matter as Democritus.

All this goes to show that the basic break with past *methods* of scientific inquiry had not taken place by the middle of the sixteenth century. It goes to show also that a great deal that is scientifically sound can be discovered without the rigorous application of what have since come to be regarded as the *methods* essential to the attainment of any scientific *proof*.

Visions derived from theology and art helped to advance scientific knowledge. So did methods and impressions derived from observation and experiment, as these had already been employed before our era, particularly by the Greeks, as these were employed again by Europeans in the twelfth and thirteenth centuries, and yet again in the fifteenth and early sixteenth centuries, with greater enthusiasm for nature and the human body than medieval persons had experienced. All these means of inquiry were at the disposal of the Europeans in the mid-sixteenth century, and knowledge of the physical and biological world would almost certainly have advanced greatly after the achievements of Copernicus, Fernel and Vesalius without the application of new methods. But it could not have advanced in the ways it has with the visions and methods that were alone available when they died. What has led in recent times to the astounding speeding up of scientific discovery and to the attainment of the immensely detailed and precise knowledge of matter, space, time and motion, including knowledge of bodily processes —plant, animal and human—such as no societies ever possessed before, has been essentially new approaches to scientific inquiry.

Perhaps it can be agreed that the scientific revolution was brought about essentially by changes in rational procedures of three principal kinds. Some scientists and historians of science today would be inclined to put first among them the novel emphasis that was placed on quantitative measurements as a basis for reaching conclusions. A classic instance of this procedure and its value in establishing new, more accurate theories of motion was the verification of the general truth of the Copernican astronomy and the correction of its serious mistakes by Tycho Brahe and Kepler. Brahe seems to have been the first modern scientist to insist on the crucial importance of accurate quantitative measurement, the first who consciously studied methods of estimating and correcting errors of observation in order to determine their limits of accuracy. In the astronomical records which he recorded on an island in the Danish Sound he attained the minimum theoretical limits of accuracy for instruments such as he used. The originality of his method and the extent to which he broke with previous European experience are shown by the fact that his most accurate predecessors were not Europeans but astronomers who worked in an observatory founded in the Near East about 1420.[1] It was because Brahe went beyond those Arabs in precision that Kepler was able, on the basis of Brahe's observations, to show that the movement of the heavenly bodies was elliptical and not circular, as Copernicus had supposed.

His measurements were more accurate than those of the Arabs. His were just accurate enough to provide Kepler, who was not mainly an extraordinarily accurate observer but, above all, an inventive mathematician, with the material needed to formulate a much more durable scientific statement: the famous 'first law' of planetary motion. According to Hall, this is 'the first instance in the history of science of a discovery being made as the result of a search for a theory, not merely to cover a given set of observations, but to interpret

[1] A. R. Hall, *The Scientific Revolution, 1500-1800* (London, 1954), pp. 118-19.

a group of refined measurements whose probable accuracy was a significant factor'.[1]

An intense concern with the reduction of the margin of quantitative error, similar to that manifested in the reconstruction of the calendar, was being applied at much the same time in the discovery and formulation of new laws in astronomy and physics. The chief instrument which enabled Brahe to go beyond the Arabs in accuracy was the telescope. Both the telescope and the microscope were apparently invented in Europe about 1580. The interest in a closer examination of the distant and the small, which brought about these inventions, is an illustration of the desire to obtain more accurate measurements as a result of increasing curiosity in matters mainly of scientific interest. It resembled the increasing concern over speeding up all arithmetical operations with the help of new calculating devices for more immediately practical purposes.

The movement in scientific inquiry to measure more accurately, and to measure phenomena which had not been measured before, to measure the speed of sound and of light, as Galileo was attempting to do, was inseparable from another innovation of the late sixteenth and early seventeenth centuries in Europe. Observation and experiment were not new; Aristotle had experimented. What was new was the insistence on observation and experiment as the only valid proof of any scientific proposition. Concepts derived from theology or from art were no longer treated as true until they had been positively verified by the senses. Such insistence on tangible proofs hardly goes back beyond the times of William Gilbert of Colchester, who was born in 1544. In his *De Magnete*, published in 1600, Gilbert wrote that there was no description or explanation in the book that he had not verified several times 'with his own eyes'.

By the times of Isaac Newton, who was born a century later than Gilbert, in 1642, the year the greatest earlier

[1] Hall, *op. cit.* p. 121.

scientific innovator, Galileo, died, it had become habitual among the leading physical scientists to insist on tangible proofs for the establishment of scientific facts and the statement of scientific laws. Schrödinger tells us that it was on the basis of the new methods in physics that Gassendi (1592–1655) and Descartes (1596–1650) revived the views of the atomistic structure of matter, put forward by the ancient Greeks, but long ignored. The new statement of atomistic structure was purged of the complication involved in the Greek claim that the soul itself was composed of atoms. In the early seventeenth century scientists had begun a separation (destined to prove extraordinarily fruitful in results) between phenomena which could be observed without calling on the resources of man's inner experience for final judgements and phenomena which are explicable, if at all, only in terms of the human personality, which cannot be understood by modern scientific methods. It is a separation between the human personality, the whole man who does the observing, and the subjects—the processes—which he attempts to describe and explain.

In the beginning this separation was not accompanied by any serious claim that the inner man is material. So there was no effort to revive the ancient Greek concept that the soul had a peculiar atomic structure of its own. (When, later on, in the eighteenth century, some scientists began to conceive of the soul as material, they assumed, unlike Democritus, that its atomic structure was in no way different from the atomic structure of matter in general.)

In the biological sciences a similar movement towards an unprecedented insistence on proof by experiment occurred at the beginning of the seventeenth century. It was exemplified above all in the work of Harvey. As the late Sir Charles Sherrington showed, the delight which we associate with the generation of Jean Fernel, Harvey's greatest European predecessor in physiology, was delight 'in natural objects and natural occurrences for their own sakes'. There was nothing fundamentally new in this kind of delight. The great Greeks had felt it. The change came nearly a century after Fernel. In Harvey's persistent pursuit of the experimental evidence obtained from the vivisection of vast numbers of animals and insects, in the face of misunderstanding and opposition, we have a novel approach to the study of the body. It consisted in what Sherrington, contrasting Harvey's work with Fernel's, called the 'new-found delight in natural observation for its own sake'.[1]

Kepler's success in working out his laws of planetary motion depended on insight that was derived not from art but from a new mathematical approach to physical phenomena. The third innovation that brought about the scientific revolution was the rise of modern mathematics. It was during the lifetime of Kepler and of Galileo that the leading scientists began to discover that the physical universe was a kind of book written in mathematical language. It was the development of mathematics at the beginning of the *seventeenth* century, as a discipline capable of almost limitless refinement, that provided the keys to this language. As Whitehead observed, 'the mathematics which now emerged into prominence', with the mathematical discoveries of Descartes, Desargues, Fermat, Roberval and Pascal, based though it frequently was on unsolved problems raised by the ancient Greeks,

was a very different science.... It...started upon its almost incredible modern career of piling subtlety of generalization upon subtlety of generalization; and of finding with each growth of complexity, some new application, either to physical science, or to philosophic thought.[2]

Mathematics, as it developed, provided what we may perhaps call a new instrument of intuition, suited better in the long run to science than to art, in that the results of the imaginative mind were susceptible to mathematical demonstration and so

---

[1] Charles Sherrington, *The Endeavour of Jean Fernel* (Cambridge, 1946), pp. 144–5.
[2] A. N. Whitehead, *Science and the Modern World* (1925), Mentor Books, 1949, p. 31.

to positive proof. This new instrument happened to correspond accurately, as Copernicus' intuition did not, with facts in the world of nature.

By means of the new mathematics, with its notions of continuous functions, of periodicity and general recurrence, intuitive insights concerning natural phenomena acquired a provable basis in the mind alone, on a very high level of abstraction. For example, the mathematical theories of periodicity made it possible for the first time to predict exactly the time of eclipses of the sun or moon and of the appearance of comets.[1] Within the realm of tangible occurrences in nature, the imaginative powers of the mind could play about henceforth with possibilities for successful, provable conclusions that were out of the question before new mathematical propositions were discovered by the French geometers. Thus the new mathematics made it possible for the first time to probe the secrets of the physical universe with no other instruments than a pencil and a piece of paper, confident that, if the mathematical argument was sound, the results were no longer merely probable but, as Descartes insisted they should be, virtually certain. A new avenue was opened to scientific explorers which had never been accessible before. 'The idea of functionality in the abstract sphere of mathematics found itself reflected in the order of nature under the guise of mathematically expressed laws of nature', Whitehead wrote. 'Apart from this progress of mathematics, the seventeenth-century developments of science would have been impossible.'[2]

On top of the notions of continuous functions and of periodicity, mathematicians—Fermat foremost among them —began to do with numbers things that had never been done before. His correspondence with Pascal beginning in 1654 suggests that their discussion of the probabilities of winning

[1] I am not suggesting that no one had successfully predicted an eclipse before this time. I am told that Thales managed to do so. But the actual systematic prediction of these movements of heavenly bodies is a modern phenomenon.

[2] Whitehead, *op. cit.* p. 32.

in a throw of dice was the genesis of the calculus of probabilities which Newton was soon after to use in setting forth a single natural physical law pervading the universe. As Jacques Chevalier, the modern editor of this correspondence, has written:

> The calculus of probabilities was of the utmost importance because it provided the basis for the mathematical theory of risk (*la théorie mathématique du hasard*), which, in our time, tends to supply the general form in which all the sciences, from physics to sociology, express their laws. As a result of this theory it is numbers, more than movements and forces, which play a decisive part in the government of nature....It enables us to penetrate more deeply than ever before the secrets of the universe....[1]

Thus the new mathematics had already developed by 1660 in those directions which have provided science ever since with its most successful methods of discovery.

In summing up the results of his historical inquiry into the 'scientific revolution' from 1500 to 1800, Dr Hall tells us that, notwithstanding the extraordinary 'growth of complexity in both theory and experimental practice...since that time,... the processes, the tactics and the forms by which modern science has evolved have not changed'.[2] The strategy of modern science was in process of formation throughout the three centuries preceding 1800. Before the processes, the tactics and the forms, of which Dr Hall speaks, were discovered, the ground had to be prepared for them. After they had been discovered, they had to be tried out and elaborated. But it was during the years from about 1570 to 1660 that they were introduced. If any period can be singled out as the one in which the language of modern science was invented and first used, that is the period. The procedures and the ways of stating scientific propositions employed by Rutherford and Einstein and Poincaré were already employed by Galileo and Kepler and Fermat. They had not been employed by their

---

[1] *L'Œuvre de Pascal*, ed. Jacques Chevalier, I (Paris, 1926), 72 ff.
[2] A. R. Hall, *The Scientific Revolution, 1500–1800*, pp. xii–xiii.

predecessors. No doubt this is what Whitehead meant when he wrote, about the age of Galileo and Kepler and Fermat, 'Since a babe was born in a manger, it may be doubted whether so great a thing has happened with so little stir'.[1]

To say so much is not to suggest that the invention of this new scientific language can be understood historically without the preparation that preceded it, without the traditions which nourished it. Its base was ancient and very broad, for the audacity with which men have used their minds in the pursuit of truth in the natural realm was derived from a view of the whole man, according to which his scientific curiosity was part of a wider search for faith and beauty, in which Truth was regarded as one and ultimately as indivisible, and relevant to all human experience. If men were to strike out in search of scientific truth in new ways, as Gilbert and Galileo and Harvey and Descartes did, they had to believe that the truth they sought was absolute. They had to have immense confidence in their rational powers, to feel certain that the results the human intellect could achieve were valid for all creation and even beyond time, that they were not simply the peculiar discoveries of men without any permanent abiding place in the universe.

This confidence was not an innovation of Galileo's age. It was derived from centuries of habit in abstract thought as the basis for durable generalizations, and this habit goes back at least as far as Aristotle. It was derived from a faith in the reality and in the dignity of pure ideas as they form in the disinterested mind without any enslavement to the realities of palpable, sensual experiences, a faith which goes back at least as far as Plato. It was derived from the powers of direct observation, demonstrated in visual form by the great art of Europe, of the East and of classical antiquity. It was derived perhaps most of all from the Christian faith, as that had been expounded especially by Aquinas and Augustine, a faith that conceived of God as the Truth, and of man, since he and he

[1] Whitehead, *op. cit.* p. 2; see also pp. 6–7.

alone is made in the image of God, as able to participate, though dimly and imperfectly, in the Truth by virtue of his intellect and also of his imagination—both the intellect and the imagination being conceived of as part of the soul, and so as basically immaterial, and by their potential union with God as indestructible and eternal. That certainty in the existence of absolute reality is what gave men the courage to read anew the book of nature, which almost every European assumed had been made by the God whom Christ revealed.

Leonardo da Vinci and Copernicus and Vesalius were reading that book anew, but they were not the discoverers of the vital new methods of reading it. They belong to what was in the main a transition period from the older science to the new sciences. Their methods of examining natural phenomena were derived mainly from the past.

This transition period was the time when the great maritime explorers opened new horizons. It was an essential preparation for modern science, and it led directly into the period of fundamental innovations in methods that followed. But it is with these fundamental innovations in methods that we are mainly concerned when we seek to discover the part which the mind has played in the genesis of industrialism, a part that is discussed at the close of the next chapter.

One is struck, in connexion with the innovations in scientific methods, by the important role played in them by quantitative precision and a new and advanced mathematical rigour—the new dimensions in abstract thought to which the great French geometers contributed so much. And this aspect of the scientific revolution leads one to ask what connexions may have existed between it and the fresh interest in quantitative accuracy, in precise quantitative statements concerning economic and political life. The increasing interest in quantitative values, the new concern of statesmen like Buckhurst and political thinkers like Bodin with rates of increase and quantitative economics occurred during the same span of years as the revolutionary innovations in scientific methods.

Movements of the Mind

The movement of the mind towards quantitative precision in connexion with the temporal world was useful to the scientists in their new adventures in abstract speculation. While the new quantitative data that were being assembled were of little direct value to them at the time, the improved methods of calculating provided them with facilities, lacking before, which helped them to obtain results of their own. Better arithmetic, as well as algebra, was an essential foundation for the development of the higher mathematics. The new experimenters with the mysteries of numbers found it highly useful to be able to add, to divide, to multiply and to subtract more quickly and efficiently; the new calculating devices liberated their minds from routine labour and helped them to concentrate on the more creative sides of mathematics.

The fact that they felt an intense and often a passionate desire so to concentrate was part of the increasing interest in quantitative matters and values that was manifesting itself in other realms. The connexion between the two was hardly one of cause and effect. Whitehead is right in a sense in suggesting that the scientific revolution began with little stir. Yet in another sense it was the expression of movements of the mind far wider in scope. The movements of the mind that were taking place in Europe during the age of religious wars, moreover, were by no means solely in the direction of quantitative precision and greater concern with the multiplication of commodities and people. These developments were accompanied by other innovations, much closer to the concerns of the heart and the imagination, to the human sides of life, than the innovations of economics and science. The movements of the mind from the late sixteenth to the mid-seventeenth centuries were also qualitative in their implications and their consequences. These consequences, in so far as they relate to the coming of industrial civilization, are the subject of the last chapters of this book. We must first consider what relations the new quantitative economic and political thinking and the scientific revolution had to the genesis of industrialism.

34

II

THE GENESIS OF INDUSTRIALISM

History is concerned with human beings. The mysterious intangible processes of imaginative thought are of all the attributes of men and women those which distinguish them most from other living creatures. What has given them their special dignity has been their search after the truth concerning themselves and their relation to the universe. Added to this have been their efforts to present images of the truth in forms that will delight the mind and senses of the beholder.

Historians, especially since the publications of Marx, have made much of the ways in which works of the mind and even of the imagination are determined by the ordinary business of life, and in particular by the material objectives and the forms of economic organization which prevail when scientists, saints, philosophers and artists are at work. Has not the spread of the supposition that our thoughts and works, as well as our acts, are historically determined, led us in recent decades to leave out of account the very element which is at the root of the greatest achievements of the mind and of the imagination (achievements which are sometimes exercised in the realm of action also), the power that men and women have to rise out of themselves, to be better than they are?

While efforts to approach the truth seem aimless in terms of daily bread and butter, these efforts have had, in the long run, an immense influence on the ways in which the daily needs of men and women have been satisfied. The changes in these ways brought about by science, by religious belief and practice, and by works of art have had an important part in determining history. I am writing these pages in the hope that the questions that have been raised in Belfast at the meetings of the Wiles Trust concerning the influence of man, in his dignity, upon the course of history since the fifteenth century, may help to make history intelligible as an effort, full though it is of set-backs and disillusionments, to serve the human soul in its glory.

I. THE RENAISSANCE AND INDUSTRIAL GROWTH

For the history of the past four hundred years in Europe a question that is of primary importance is the relation between the movements of the mind and the changes in economic and especially industrial conditions that have accompanied them. Scientists and experts in the history of science are beginning to agree that the sixteenth and seventeenth centuries were of decisive importance in the birth of modern science. But can we speak in any valid sense of the birth of industrialism during those centuries?

What was happening to industrial production in Europe between the late fifteenth century and the middle of the seventeenth? As a result of European initiative during those years, the entire world as we know it was circled in small sailing ships, mapped and thrown open to trade and to colonization. The same vision and initiative, the same daring, which led the Europeans to penetrate what were still in the fourteen-eighties untold, unattained horizons, might be expected to have manifested themselves nearer home in many domains, including the making and the marketing of commodities.

Under the spell of the quantitative data that modern scholars have assembled, the sixteenth and seventeenth centuries have been successively described as times of commercial revolution, price revolution and industrial revolution. A case can be made for all these descriptions on the basis of statistics, but there has been a disposition to make more of the changes which the statistics sometimes reveal than they will bear, and to attribute to them a deceptive novelty. I write as one of the sinners. Rates of increase in output or in trade are bound to give an impression of phenomenal rapidity when we start

from almost nothing—as we do, for example, with the manufacture of such commodities as tobacco, tobacco pipes, paper
or alum or when we actually start from nothing, as we do in
the trade with America.

We are in danger of taking a position reminiscent of one of
my countrymen on the eve of the First World War. He was
an anti-feminist. He said that since women had had the vote,
crime among them had increased 'a hundred per cent'.
Challenged for evidence, he cited the state of Wyoming,
which had been admitted recently into the Union in spite of
its sparse population, and which, among the United States,
was one of the first to pass a law granting women the suffrage.
Before the law was passed, this man pointed out, there had
been one woman in the state penitentiary. Now there were
two! So, in treating the statistical evidence of economic
growth during the hundred and fifty years that began with
the discovery of America, we must always keep in mind the
small size or volume of the base from which we start.

During the early decades of the sixteenth century, the
times of Copernicus and Erasmus, Fernel and Rabelais, the
period of the Reformation, the principal generating forces of
industrial expansion in Europe had little to do with the discovery of America.[1] They were mainly European; most of
them would have come into operation if no continent had
separated Europe and Africa from Asia. One of these forces
was a fresh interest in fashioning objects of every kind in new
styles to delight the senses. This interest had begun rather
earlier in Italy. The fine architecture of the Renaissance
developed to a considerable degree through the initiative of
Ghiberti and Brunelleschi, both of whom flourished during
the first half of the fifteenth century. The spread of this
architecture and the enthusiasm for building and rebuilding
which it helped to generate, the embellishment in new styles
of churches, of new chapels in older churches, of great houses

[1] See Nef, *La Naissance de la civilisation industrielle et le monde contemporain* (Paris,
1954), ch. v.

for municipal government and of merchants' palaces, was accompanied by the fashioning of objects of art of all kinds from oil paintings to suits of the most elegant armour.

These movements often brought with them an extension of the area claimed by towns. New town walls and bridges were erected. Building and furnishing in new styles created a new demand for larger quantities of raw materials. At the same time the introduction of new technical processes, mostly invented for artistic purposes, such as printing, crystal-glass-making, the separating of silver and copper from argentiferous copper ores with the help of lead, encouraged a multiplication of output. Between about 1460 and 1530 the production of silver and copper in central Europe apparently increased some five times over.[1] The output of paper probably grew still more rapidly. Old buildings were remodelled in scores of towns to let in the light and accommodate printing presses and the necessary supplies of movable type, and, as a result, books which had been extremely scarce became by contrast plentiful. The printed leaflets of the early Lutherans are said to have been distributed by the hundreds of thousands. In most of Europe this was a time of expanding output in mining and metallurgy, and in the production of durable commodities. It was a time also of expanding trade and agriculture. It was a time of increasing population in Italy, Spain, France, the Low Countries, southern Germany and central Europe generally.

The interest taken by Europeans in a multiplication of commodities was less in multiplication for its own sake, for the sake of spreading cheap conveniences among a larger proportion of the population, than in multiplication for certain purposes, non-economic in their inspiration. Pamphlets advocating reform were wanted in as large numbers as possible, in order that they might lead hosts of persons of every class to follow Luther in his religious discipline, which proved to be one road to Protestantism. Religion had long been regarded

---

[1] Nef, 'Silver production in central Europe', *Journal of Political Economy*, XLIX (1941), 586.

as the affair of everyone. By distributing as many pamphlets as possible, religious leaders were only employing new means in the service of an end which had been in the forefront of western European life for a great many centuries, ever since the advent of Christianity. Its basic mission was to bring salvation to as many souls as possible. The fact that there was greater division of opinion than ever before as to the means of doing so did not diminish the intensity with which this mission was pursued. For a time it increased the intensity.[1]

A great variety of concepts derived from art and faith had directed the work of the Europeans earlier in the Middle Ages in the fashioning of durable objects and commodities, from cathedrals and crucifixes to windows, chests and furniture. In the times of Erasmus and Copernicus also, concepts derived from the same sources prevailed, but the sphere of art was greatly extended. The artists devoted themselves less exclusively than they had to religious subjects. It is perhaps no exaggeration to say that the chief force behind the employment of labour and the investment of capital was delight in artistic perfection. At the same time, the raw materials available were increasing in number—for example alum for dyeing and calamine for making brass were exploited profusely for the first time. Where it seemed possible not to sacrifice beauty in the objects produced, there was sometimes a notable increase in the quantity and also in the variety of commodities. This was the case with etchings and wood-cuts and printed books. But one cannot multiply etchings or wood-cuts or the finest editions indefinitely without losing touch with the hand of the artists. This the principal producers of Renaissance Europe were unwilling to do.

New houses went up, reservoirs were built to store water for towns, more bridges spanned the moving rivers along which most European towns were built, without spoiling the older beauty of the many cities which had clustered about the

[1] Compare Lucien Febvre, *Le Problème de l'incroyance au XVIe siècle: la religion de Rabelais* (Paris, 1947), p. 500.

cathedrals and churches of the eleventh, twelfth and thirteenth centuries. A rich diversity was achieved within a general harmony of architectural design. This was not the result of town planning in the modern sense, with its subways and auto highways, its railroads and air terminals, its sewage disposal and transmission of power and heat. The diversity of Renaissance towns and villages was derived from a common aesthetic inspiration concerning what was architecturally fitting, generated partly by the models of classical antiquity and partly by a fresh curiosity concerning nature and the ways of using nature as material for art.

In some respects this movement to build and to fashion in new styles works of art in greater profusion was not in the direction of satisfying a larger number of persons. The greatest building enterprises of the twelfth and thirteenth centuries had been the cathedrals and the principal churches, with their almost infinitely elaborate decorations, from stained glass windows to myriad statues. The great Romanesque and Gothic churches which the tourist now visits, belonged in a real sense to all the local inhabitants, in an age when everyone was at least nominally a communicant. Sumptuous palaces had been erected at great expense for private merchants in the thirteenth and early fourteenth centuries, notably in the largest Italian towns, especially in Florence. But it was hardly until the mid-fifteenth century that a very large share of all expenditures on building in most European towns began to be devoted to the houses of merchant princes, to the town halls and *palais de justice* of municipal governments in which the mercantile elements had often predominant power. Thus the change in styles of architecture, and the development of the visual arts in new forms and with new materials, tended to coincide with changes in the clientele for building.

This contrast between the older Romanesque or Gothic building and Renaissance building can be seen in the ancient, compact, entrancing town of Bourges. In a sort of saucer in the lower part of the city rises one of the most beautiful of medieval cathedrals. Not far off, up a slowly rising hill, leaning flush against a narrow, slightly curving street, is the palace of Jacques Cœur—the richest and most glamorous French merchant of the fifteenth century. The cathedral was built, in the main, during the late twelfth and thirteenth centuries. Jacques Cœur's palace went up two or three hundred years afterwards, in a much briefer space of time, during the decade of the fourteen-forties.

The cathedral is a world in itself. It has come down to us much as it was in the thirteenth century, with statues in stone and incomparable stained-glass windows, cut and fashioned to instruct the people in morality and beauty, to strengthen them in their faith and to console them in their temporal lives. By comparison the palace of Jacques Cœur, for all its harmony and symmetry, for all its perfection as a work of art and as a setting for works of art, seems obsolete and barren. Erected for the purposes of one man rather than for all the faithful, its *raison d'être*, unlike that of the cathedral, disappeared ages ago. It was once full of rich chests and beds, exquisite ornamental iron, gold and silver work. The interior walls were decorated with painted-glass windows and wonderful tapestries. In the rooms were curious pieces of sculpture, some of them hidden in ample closets reached only by a concealed staircase. The bedding was sumptuous. The dining tables were once set with the finest service in gold and silver. Among the most perfect of all French fifteenth-century buildings, the palace was for a few years full of the luxurious, exciting life led by Jacques Cœur and his friends and associates, including some of the most powerful officials in France. After the rich merchant's disgrace and imprisonment, his palace was confiscated by the French crown in 1453. It has since passed through the hands of many persons including (two hundred years afterwards) the great Colbert, whose rise from humble origins to the highest offices in the state resembled superficially the rise of Cœur himself. Eventually the building was taken over by the municipal government.

In the course of time it was stripped of many of its interior decorations and of all its original purpose. Now it is a museum.

Merchants' palaces, of which Jacques Cœur's is an example, enlarged the circle of private participants in beautiful commodities. But the circle of participants was very much smaller than that which shared directly in the beauties of Romanesque and Gothic cathedrals and churches. It was much more exclusive.

It was to some extent the same with Renaissance religious structures. There was a concentration upon the installation of chapels, constructed mainly to provide a place of worship for a few individuals. So Renaissance building (and the industrial expansion which accompanied it) was hardly a movement in the direction of the mass consumption which is characteristic of the recent industrialized age. The common citizen in the towns had a much less direct stake in the new palaces than his ancestors had in the old churches and cathedrals.

It is not difficult to represent the growth of trade and of industrial enterprise, which was impressive in the times of Leonardo da Vinci and Erasmus, as leading in the direction of the present industrialized world. In the sense in which it was from out of this Europe—the Europe of the Renaissance —that modern Europe came, such a connexion is obvious. The same thing can be said of the development of economic life in Europe from the mid-eleventh to the early fourteenth century. All the great past experiences of the Europeans, including their contacts with antiquity and with the civilizations of the East, can easily be led to seem, in the light of what has happened since, a preparation for industrialism.

So they were. In the same way the development of scientific thought in classical and medieval times, and especially in the times of Copernicus and Vesalius, was a preparation for the scientific revolution. But the methods and objectives of earlier scientists did not make modern science inevitable in the same way that the innovations in thought of the period from roughly 1570 to 1660 made it inevitable. Were there innovations in that same period of which the same thing can be said in connexion with industrial history? Did developments which took place during the late sixteenth and early seventeenth centuries make modern industrialism inevitable in a sense that earlier developments of the age of the Renaissance and of the age of Romanesque and Gothic art did not?

2. THE REFORMATION AND THE WEAKENING OF DESPOTISM *c.* 1540–*c.* 1640

A notable feature of economic history during the span of years when the human mind was striking out in new directions towards modern science, was the shift that occurred in the centres of prosperity, both in trade and industry, from southern Europe and the Continent generally to the north, to lands reclaimed from the sea in the United Provinces, and above all to the Scandinavian peninsula and the island of Great Britain. The expansion of production and of trade in many parts of Europe from about 1460 to 1550 came to an end in most continental countries during the last half of the sixteenth century or at the beginning of the seventeenth. In central Europe and Spain the prosperity associated with the Renaissance was followed by a long period of declining output. Such a decline seems to have begun in Hungary, and to have spread to Austria, Bohemia, Poland, eastern and southern Germany during the second half of the sixteenth century. In Spain and in Franche-Comté, which was under Spanish dominion, such a decline seems to have begun at the end of Philip II's reign, which is to say in the fifteen-nineties. In all these countries the decline lasted through the Thirty Years War, which tended to accentuate it.

Great Britain had participated less than most continental countries in the industrial development of the Renaissance. Rapid growth of industrial output during the reign of Henry VII and the early years of the reign of Henry VIII was largely confined to one area, the south-west, where the textile industry thrived and where large fortunes were made in the trade in wool and cloth. The progress of mining and metallurgy was unimpressive compared with that of central Europe. In 1539 a correspondent of Thomas Cromwell's described the lead mines of England as 'dead'. While the output of tin—the great staple of English mining in the Middle Ages—increased some sixty or seventy per cent between 1470 and 1540, such a rate of growth was slow compared with that in the production of almost all metals in central Europe. The earlier supremacy of the tin of Devon and Cornwall in continental European markets was threatened by the progress of tin mining in Spain, Portugal, Saxony, Bavaria and Bohemia.[1]

A striking growth in production, which characterized so much of continental Europe in the late fifteenth century and at the beginning of the sixteenth, hardly began in England before the reign of Henry VIII. It hardly became impressive until the decade of the fifteen-forties when Henry VIII died. The development in England, which came later than in the continental countries, had certain features which were peculiar to the north, which were shared by Scotland, by Sweden and to some extent by Holland.

The Reformation was accompanied everywhere by a movement of European rulers to confiscate monastic properties, but it was only in the states which broke definitely with Rome, especially in England and Wales, in Scotland, Sweden and Holland, that this movement was a complete success. As a result, the Church had much less to spend in those countries, the proportion of the population which gained its living from the care of souls was greatly reduced, and, after the rise of Protestantism and Calvinism in particular, with its condemnation of saints and images, austerity in connexion with churches and religious ceremonies became a virtue.[2] All these

[1] Nef, 'Industrial Europe at the time of the Reformation', *Journal of Political Economy*, XLIX (1941), 222.
[2] Nef, 'La Riforma Protestante e l'origine della civiltà industriale', *Economia e Storia*, II (1955), 18 ff.

changes meant a substantial alteration in the relation of the religious to the economic life. For centuries the Church, not least through the monasteries and the practises of monasticism, had contributed to the formation of taste by its expenditures, particularly its orders for building and for works of art. Through the control exercised by the clergy—as the recipients of charitable gifts, as the owners of land and mineral resources, as tax collectors and financiers, as investors in partnerships for the production and trade of wool and silk and cloth, of ores and metals and alum—the Church had contributed to the ways in which capital and labour were employed in every part of Europe. Persons in religious orders, from the pope to the abbots and priors who managed monastic estates, had an immense influence upon both economic demand and economic supply. This influence was of hardly less importance during the decades that preceded the Reformation than it had been in the centuries of developing Romanesque and Gothic architecture.

To represent all these religious orders and ecclesiastical foundations as having a single coherent attitude or policy towards the use of the resources they controlled, towards investments in land or buildings, towards the purchase of raw materials and commodities, the employment of labour, towards workmanship, would be grotesque. It would be equally grotesque to suggest that there was no change from generation to generation in the attitude of the religious or the lay clergy towards their religious functions and the economic functions which accompanied them. The Roman Church is a body made up of individual human beings with great diversity of outlook and of experience. All of them are swayed, but in enormously varying degrees and ways, by the experiences of the temporal world and by historical changes, for even the most cloistered monk or nun is never completely disembodied. Can we then speak of the Church as having any specific kinds of influences on the kinds of commodities produced?

45

Only in a very general way can we speak so. The chief function of the Roman clergy was the saving of souls, their own and other people's. The tangible means of saving souls, according to ecclesiastical practice, were various, but the central means was the administration of the sacraments, and, for the religious, the practice of the monastic life. In order to carry out these functions, the clergy regarded it as essential to construct, maintain and renew cathedrals, churches and monasteries, to supply them with the necessary ingredients for administering the sacraments, to provide the ornaments and images of sacred art. The clergy were in this way committed to the kind of economic development in which the production of works of art and craftsmanship was the central objective.

In so far as the Reformation eliminated the clergy, or substituted for the older clergy a new clergy with different functions, the religious stimulus to an economy oriented towards art and craftsmanship was withdrawn. This is just what was happening in Great Britain (in Scotland as well as in England and Wales) during the sixteenth and seventeenth centuries. Professor Baskerville's work warns us against exaggerating the abruptness of the change effected by the acts of dissolution of 1536 and 1539. Before the Reformation, he shows, laymen had taken over part of the economic functions performed by the monks in many manors or sections of manors belonging to ecclesiastical foundations. Most of the religious eliminated by the acts were not persecuted but pensioned off.

Nevertheless the substitution for the Roman of the Anglican Church, without any monastic life and with a married clergy, was accompanied by an enormous shrinkage in the revenue available for ecclesiastical purposes in England and in the proportion of the population employed directly in the service of the Christian faith. The money for the upkeep of cathedrals and churches was most inadequate, especially during the early seventeenth century. With the rise of Puritanism and Presbyterianism at that time, efforts were made within both the Church of England and the Church of Scotland to eliminate images and other decorations from the places of worship, or at least not to install further images and decorations. While this did not produce an austerity comparable to that which we find in the Calvinist temples of France, the lukewarm enthusiasm of the low church for music and coloured glass and ornament did not help the high clergy to press for the funds needed for the renewal in England of sacred art. Both the will and the means to continue the demands for works of beauty which characterized the Roman Church were much weaker in England.

Meanwhile the lands once in the possession of the monasteries and lesser religious gilds (many of them rich in mineral resources, particularly coal and iron ore) passed at the dissolution from ecclesiastical ownership. A considerable portion of these lands went almost at once to private persons, noblemen and merchants, to persons who were rich enough to buy them, or who had influence enough to receive them as a reward for services to the sovereign. Before the Civil War the crown, hard pressed for funds, had disposed of virtually all the remaining lands that had once belonged to the monasteries, and a good deal of royal property besides.[1]

This widespread transfer of lands meant that new landed proprietors, who were frequently governed by different economic motives, replaced religious foundations much more often than in those countries where the Roman Catholic Church retained its authority. There was a greater personal incentive to amass capital in the form of individual savings among private individuals with heirs than among monks and priests who thought and behaved as members of ecclesiastical institutions. In search of profits, the new proprietors were generally more disposed than the old to take financial risks. So, where there was the possibility of exploiting mineral wealth in iron ore or coal or of planting new crops such as hops or tobacco, these proprietors were either more eager

[1] Nef, *Industry and Government in France and England, 1540–1640* (Philadelphia, 1940), p. 128.

than their religious predecessors to invest heavily on their own account in new industrial enterprises, which required costly equipment, or were more willing to lease the land and subsoil they owned on terms that were likely to attract wealthy economic adventurers—city men and others. During the seventeenth and eighteenth centuries, in France and England and perhaps almost everywhere in Europe, the most heavily capitalized and productive mining and metallurgical enterprises appear to have been in lands owned by the laity.[1] In Great Britain and probably elsewhere the terms on which leases could be obtained were more attractive to investors where the land was in private hands than where it belonged to the Church.[2]

A movement towards political absolutism, which had characterized the history of continental Europe in the times of Erasmus and Copernicus, did not come to an end in most European states with the Reformation. It continued through the seventeenth century and even beyond, though the most despotic and cruel features of Renaissance princely government were considerably mitigated even before the end of the Thirty Years War, particularly in France. During the same period, the first half of the seventeenth century, the times of Galileo and Descartes, the aristocracy (the ancient landed families) gained in wealth and political influence, especially in Italy and in France.

These movements were accompanied by an increase in the authority exercised by the Crown in France over industrial development, not only through the regulation of work and the establishment of royal manufactures, but through the increase in the royal revenue. In all these respects English history during the late sixteenth and the first half of the seventeenth centuries diverged from continental and particularly from French history. In England the effectiveness of the economic regulations of the Crown and of its participation in

[1] Nef, *The United States and Civilization* (Chicago, 1942), pp. 158-9.
[2] Nef, *The Rise of the British Coal Industry*, II (London, 1932), 135-56.

manufactures diminished. At the same time the royal revenue, which had increased notably under Henry VII and Henry VIII, hardly grew at all in terms of actual purchasing power during the reigns of Elizabeth I, James I and Charles I. Meanwhile the real revenue of the French crown had at least doubled. Taxes in England on the eve of the Civil War came to something like 2s. 6d. per head, only about a fourth as much as in France.[1]

The bearing of the very different history of political authority in the two countries upon the course of economic development is similar to that of the very different history of ecclesiastical authority. In France the policy of government regulation, and especially of government participation in industry, was pushed farthest in the spheres in which the policy of princes had conflicted least with the objectives of economic enterprise, in the fashioning by trained hand labour of the finest luxury articles and works of art, such as tapestries and oil paintings. Financial policy worked in the same direction, to favour an economy in which the motives of the artist and the artisan were foremost. Taxes fell almost entirely on the third estate, and this tended to concentrate large blocks of spending and investing power in the crown and the aristocracy, as well as in the clergy. The rich nobles who gathered about the court, or who maintained small courts of their own in the provinces, laid out much of the money which they did not give to support the new charitable religious orders, on beautiful buildings and exquisite furniture, musical instruments and other works of art.[2]

Ecclesiastical and constitutional history did not determine the course taken by industrial development during the late sixteenth and the early seventeenth centuries. But the shrinkage in the financial power and in the authority of both Church and Crown in the north of Europe and particularly in Great Britain, created a kind of economic vacuum.

[1] Nef, *Industry and Government in France and England*, pp. 126–8.
[2] *Ibid.* pp. 139–42.

That made it easier there to rewrite industrial history afresh than in countries where the Roman Church or the reigning prince, or both, retained their full power and authority. How was industrial history being written in the north, particularly in Great Britain? What was the relation of the new orientation of the human mind, which was so striking during the same period, to the course of industrial history?

3. TOWARDS A QUANTITATIVE ECONOMY

After the dissolution of the English monasteries, a novel tendency in the direction of an economy devoted primarily to the production of cheap wares in ever larger quantities manifested itself in the north of Europe and above all in Great Britain. This tendency was accentuated at the end of the sixteenth century. It was associated especially with a new and extensive use of cast and pig iron and coal fuel.[1]

The significance for industrialism of the changing nature of iron metallurgy in the north of Europe did not consist mainly in the movement towards larger iron-making establishments. It consisted rather in the orientation of the iron-making industry away from products wanted primarily for their beauty and durability, in the direction of products wanted primarily for their utility. In the older metallurgical processes, where wrought iron had been produced directly from the ore by repeated heating and hammering on the anvil, large quantities of metal were lost as slag and scale. Now that the ores were melted, these losses were materially reduced. It became economical to exploit cheap ores, in which Great Britain abounded. Liquid iron was cast into such articles as kitchen pots and pans, and into cannon which were apparently first successfully produced with this metal in Sussex. The

---

[1] For the earlier use made in China of cast and pig iron and coal, see my *La Naissance de la civilisation industrielle et le monde contemporain* (Paris, 1954).

For the growth of the output of cast and pig iron in England, see Nef, 'Note on the progress of iron production in England, 1540–1640', *Journal of Political Economy*, XLIV (1936), 398 ff.

standardized bars and rods obtained at the new forges and slitting mills, from the pig-like blocks brought from the blast furnaces, served the nailer or the blacksmith better than the craftsman who fashioned iron balustrades, ornamental locks and keys and iron tracery for doors and strong-boxes, or the craftsman who fashioned suits of armour or elegant firearms.

The pressure for cheaper fuel in Great Britain brought about an unprecedented development of coal resources. While the reign of Elizabeth II seems to mark the end of English supremacy among the nations of the world in the exploitation of coal, the reign of Elizabeth I marked the beginning.

Until after the Reformation, until about the middle of the sixteenth century, the small principality of Liège was probably more productive of coal than any county or shire in Great Britain. Liège coal was not quite carried to Newcastle. But coal shipped thence down the Meuse competed with Newcastle coal at Calais and other Channel ports in the reign of Henry VIII. The local market for coal in Liège was then probably greater than that in any city in Great Britain.

By the time of the English Civil War all this had changed. With the concentration of population and manufactures in London, the city alone probably consumed more coal than was mined in all the Low Countries, in the fields about Liège, Mons and Charleroi combined. Foreign visitors were astonished by the smoke from tens of thousands of domestic fires and from hundreds of workshops. With its breweries, its soap and starch houses, its brick kilns, sugar refineries, earthenware works and glass furnaces, London seemed to them hardly fit for human habitation. Londoners themselves were startled by the growth of foul-smelling manufactures, by the stench from coal-burning furnaces. Some of them complained that the fumes from an alum factory were poisoning the fish in the Thames.[1] Even John Evelyn, who took a great interest in what was called 'improvement' (which included

---

[1] *Calendar of State Papers, Domestic, 1627–8*, pp. 269–70.

the reduction of labour costs in the interest of expanding output), was repelled by the fog of smoke belching from the sooty throats of new manufacturing shops to hang over the metropolis and insinuate itself along the streets. He compared this new, darker London to 'the picture of Troy sacked by the Greeks, or the approaches of Mount-Hecla'.[1]

The shift from charcoal and wood to coal worked to a greater degree than the spread of blast furnaces in iron-making to orient the economy of Great Britain in the direction of cheap common wares. Hard coal, especially the cannel coal of Lancashire, might be used occasionally as material for fashioning commodities of some beauty and durability—such as ink-wells, statues and the floors of castles. Here in small quantities was material to arouse the ingenuity of craftsmen and builders. Such curious uses for coal were soon forgotten in the new seas of smoke. What was most obnoxious about the fuel was the damage its introduction was doing, not only to sensitive nostrils and skins, but to the quality of the materials which came in contact with its flames in the ovens and furnaces of manufacturers. In some cases, as in glass-making between about 1605 and 1610, it was necessary to invent new furnaces and new processes of manufacture in order to make possible the use of mineral fuel. The raw materials were heated in closed crucibles, to prevent all contact with the noxious fumes and flames of the burning coals. While this invention made easy the production of sheet glass—serviceable for such commodities as plain window-panes—in larger quantities than ever before, it made impracticable the blowing of glass in the flames, an art in which the Italians, and, under Italian influence, most continental peoples excelled. 'Persons of any condition are authorized to make window panes,' wrote a French *intendant* in 1700, 'à la différence des verres qui sont affectés aux gentilshommes.'[2]

[1] John Evelyn, *Fumifugium; or the Inconveniency of the Aer and Smoke of London dissipated* (1661), p. ii.
[2] *Correspondance des contrôleurs généraux des finances avec les intendants des provinces*, ed. A. M. de Boislisle, II (Paris, 1874–97), 59.

Towards a quantitative economy

By the mid-seventeenth century, partly as a result of the growing use of cast and pig iron and coal, England had obtained a lead over all other countries in the production of common commodities, in which quantity and utility rather than quality and elegance were the main concern of the makers and the consumers. In the sixteen-twenties a member of the House of Commons, which was full of rich burghers whose tastes were similar to those of the ancient aristocracy, greeted with dismay a bill to promote the wearing of native cloth. 'It is hard', he said, 'to make a law whereby we shall not know our wives from our chambermaids.'[1] Between the Reformation and the Civil War England gained an enormous absolute advantage over France in the output of such materials and commodities as coal, beer and alum. England was manufacturing, relative to her population, a larger volume of iron, copper and brass, of finished metal commodities, and of building materials such as bricks and lime. She had begun to rival France in the production of cheap paper suitable for wrapping.[2]

The orientation of industrial enterprise in the north of Europe in new directions, helped to turn the minds of businessmen towards the possibility of finding wider markets for the sale of manufactured goods at a profit. Production for a larger public became a main objective of manufacturers, mining adventurers and of the financiers who lent them money.

Economic efforts were moving in this way in the direction of the industrialism of the contemporary world. Yet the multiplication in the output of cheap wares (stimulated by the wider use of cast and pig iron and by the first general use of coal as fuel) was by no means the chief development which gave the period from about 1570 to 1660 its significance for the rise and ultimate triumph of industrialism. The greatest innovations were in the realm of the mind, in connexion with

---

[1] E. Lipson, *The Economic History of England*, III (London, 1931), 45.
[2] Nef, 'A comparison of industrial growth in France and England from 1540 to 1640', *Journal of Political Economy*, XLIV, no. 3 (1936), 663.

technology and above all with science. What was destined to revolutionize human endeavour was not so much the new technical problems of abridging manual labour which were solved in this age as the new technical problems which were raised by the introduction of a coal-burning economy. The inventive ingenuity, which these problems aroused, led eventually towards the wholesale exploitation of iron ores and new sources of power and towards the general use of machinery. But the new sense of urgency for abridging labour born of the early industrial revolution would not by itself have brought about the technological revolutions of the past hundred and fifty years. Those have been mainly a result of the new intellectual methods introduced in connexion with the natural sciences during the period from about 1570 to 1660. It was the innovations of resourceful human minds which made this period so decisive for the future of all the peoples of the world. These innovations are at the root of the single economic and political universe that confronts man in the second half of the twentieth century.

4. TOWARDS MODERN TECHNOLOGY

In technology, but not in science, men's minds focused on certain practical problems, largely as a result of the progress of a quantitative economy in Great Britain. Wood had been the basic fuel everywhere in Europe during the Middle Ages. The expansion of shipbuilding and other manufactures, the growth in population and the accompanying demand for houses and construction work of many kinds in England, Wales and Scotland, put a heavy pressure upon the forests both for fuel and for lumber.

Parts of Great Britain were relatively poor in woodlands compared with France or Germany or Sweden. An Englishman named Anthony Welldon, who was somewhat deficient in his appreciation of the Scots and their country, remarked in 1618 that if Judas had betrayed Christ in Scotland, he would have had difficulty in finding a tree on which to hang. Whether from a want of woodlands or from the rising demand for trees and shrubberies, the timber shortage had become serious by the beginning of the seventeenth century. This was true even in south Wales, where the growth of industry and population was slight compared with that in south-eastern England. Owen, the contemporary historian of Pembrokeshire, wrote in 1603, 'this Countrie groneth with the generalle complainte of other countries of the decreasinge of wood'.[1]

It was above all in London, and in the area about that fast-growing city, that problems produced by deforestation had become acute. An agent, who collected the revenues which the Bishop of London derived from his estates in Middlesex, complained about this in 1598. While earlier bishops had obtained yearly profits of from £400 to £2500 by selling their wood to London traders, he wrote, 'the nowe Bishop hathe been driven to bestowe at the least £220 in tymber for the necessary repayring of his houses, and is nowe driven to burne seacoles'.[2] It was the necessity of hauling logs long distances, or finding a substitute for them, that was mainly responsible for the wholesale adoption of coal in London and in small centres of industry and population, such as Nottingham and Coventry. As the prices of firewood and of many kinds of lumber had apparently risen by the end of Elizabeth I's reign in the capital more than the prices of any other commodity,[3] the plight in higher costs of production of some manufacturers who kept on using wood could be grievous. The alternatives were to move to the forests or to substitute coal for firewood and charcoal.

Prospective ironmasters were faced with this dilemma at the juncture of the sixteenth and seventeenth centuries. It *was* a dilemma, because the establishment of the blast furnaces with their forges in those parts of the country where wood was

[1] Owen, *Description of Pembrokeshire*, pt. I, pp. 86, 145–6.

[2] *State Papers Domestic, Elizabeth*, CCLXVI, no. 119.

[3] Nef, 'Prices and industrial capitalism in France and England', *Economic History Review*, VII, no. 2 (1937), 180–1.

plentiful provided only a temporary solution. Unlike firewood and lumber in the centres of population, charcoal for the furnaces of the metallurgists was not rising in price much more rapidly than other commodities. It was made, and mainly consumed, near the places where the trees were felled. Parts of England had abundant woodlands, and the iron-masters moved there because the same areas were often especially rich in the cheap iron ores which they wanted. 'Nature has thought fit to produce this wasting ore more plentifully in woodlands than any other ground, and to enrich our forests to their own destruction,'[1] wrote John Evelyn in a book published in 1664. By that time the output of iron in England, which had grown rapidly between the Reformation and the Civil War, was no longer increasing. The native supply was being supplemented by imports of bar iron, especially from Sweden.

Some 200 years elapsed between the time at which the technical problem of substituting coal for wood fuel was first raised in an acute form and the effective union of coal and iron. The advent of a coal-burning economy in Great Britain at the juncture of the sixteenth and seventeenth centuries was a necessary preliminary. The coming of that economy relieved to some extent the pressure on the English forests for firewood and charcoal, and so helped to give the older wood-burning iron industry a new lease on life. But the growing need which arose for importing bar iron from abroad showed that the future of iron-making in Great Britain would depend on the adoption of coal fuel. The experiments made from the early seventeenth century onwards in substituting coal for wood in many other industries provided inventors with a wide range of experiences upon which they were able to draw for the knowledge needed to solve eventually the especially difficult and complicated problems of iron metallurgy.

The need which arose at the juncture of the sixteenth and

---

[1] Evelyn, *Sylva*, as quoted John Holland, *The History and Description of Fossil Fuel* (London, 1835), p. 323.

seventeenth centuries for digging and moving coal in far greater quantities than ever before raised with an urgency that was new at least two other technical problems whose solution precipitated the industrial revolution 200 years afterwards. One was the drainage of mines at considerable depths. By the end of the sixteenth century, some persons in England began to recognize that the early sources of power (wind, water and horse power) exploited for hundreds of years in Europe for driving machinery, would prove inadequate for meeting the age-old problem of draining flooded pits in the new forms which it presented as a result of the rise of the British coal industry. It had long been realized that power might be generated by a jet of steam. At the beginning of the seventeenth century, several persons set about to try to apply this force to the drainage of coal mines. As in the case of the substitution of coal for charcoal in iron metallurgy, the problem proved to be a tough one, and it was not solved for a long time. One colliery engineer remarked a century later that the man who discovered a practical steam engine to help the mine owners was sure to be rewarded sufficiently to set up in London with his coach-and-six.

He had hardly made this remark when primitive steam engines put in their first appearance at coal mines in Staffordshire. They spread thence during the second and third decades of the eighteenth century to many mining districts in England, and also to Scotland and to the Continent. There, for the first time, industrial enterprise was beginning to be pursued with great intensity for the sake of cheaper quantitative production, *à l'imitation de l'Angleterre*, as some Frenchmen expressed it. After another fifty years of preparation, after the application in the seventeen-eighties of Watt's invention of a rotary engine, steam power came into use with a rush for driving machinery in manufactures. Some necessary preliminaries for Watt's success are to be found in the unsuccessful, but novel efforts of a number of obscure inventors of the early seventeenth century, who were spurred on by the new practical problems of drainage raised by the expansion of the coal industry.

That early expansion also created a new need for cheaper transportation overground. Coal was a commodity bulky to handle and of small value in proportion to its volume. It had often to be delivered, like firewood, at considerable distances from the source of supplies. While much greater potential heat could be concentrated in a small volume of coals than in an equal volume of logs, while coal was less cumbersome to move than wood, its substitution for wood at the chief centres of population, especially London, involved the movement of ever larger quantities overland from the pits to navigable water. Between 1597 and 1606 the first efforts were made to develop a new method of haulage. Wooden rails were fastened to the ground from collieries at Wollaton to the river Trent and from collieries at Broseley to the river Severn.[1] These rails were apparently laid along an inclined way for a distance of some miles, so that wagons loaded with coal would, by the force of their own weight, run along them to the wharves where the river ships were loaded. Then the empty wagons were hauled back on the rails by horses to the pits. The use of 'tylting rails', as they were called at the beginning of the seventeenth century in Shropshire, was apparently an English invention, prompted by the novel need for moving a cheap dirty commodity in ever increasing quantities. By the early eighteenth century 'wagon ways' of this kind provided a common means for hauling coal to the rivers and harbours in all the principal coalfields of Great Britain. They were introduced at that time into Germany, where they were called 'englischer Kohlen wegen'.[2]

These three developments were of capital importance in bringing about the industrial revolution which began in

---

[1] *H.M.C. Report on the MSS. of Lord Middleton*, p. 169; *Star Chamber Proceedings James I*, 109/8; 310/16.
[2] Ludwig Beck, *Geschichte des Eisen*, III (Braunschweig, 1884–1903), 960.

Great Britain in the seventeen-eighties.[1] The wholesale use of coal in iron metallurgy made possible the multiplication of iron and eventually of steel for machine parts and for construction work of many kinds. Steam-driven engines, when applied to manufacturing as well as to mining, led men a long way in the direction of the machine economy characteristic of industrialism. Traction on rails, when combined with the steam engine for haulage, transformed both the movement of freight and the movement of travellers overland. All these developments had their origins in the new technical problems confronting British industry at the juncture of the sixteenth and seventeenth centuries.

There are, then, grounds for speaking of an early industrial revolution in the north of Europe, and particularly in Great Britain. They do not rest on statistics of increasing output, impressive though such statistics sometimes are. They do not rest on the growth in the scale of industrial enterprise, though there was a remarkable increase in the scale at this time in many industries, from mining and metallurgy to the manufacture of alum and brewing. They rest on a novel movement during the late sixteenth and early seventeenth centuries, especially in Great Britain, towards a concentration of industrial enterprise upon the production of cheap commodities in large quantities. Both in the tastes it generated and the technical problems it raised, the early industrial revolution prepared the way for the later and more celebrated industrial revolution at the juncture of the eighteenth and nineteenth centuries.

If, as suggested at the beginning of this chapter, history is concerned with human beings, it is changes in the values which men and women attach to life, changes in the purposes to which they devote their minds and bodies in their daily work, that are of decisive importance in orienting economic

[1] See Nef, 'The Industrial Revolution reconsidered', *War and Human Progress* (London, 1951), ch. xv.

endeavour in new directions. In these respects the decades from about 1580 to 1640 *were* a turning point. It was then that persons in the north of Europe, and particularly in Great Britain, began to lay an emphasis on utility as the goal of industrial life—on productivity as a self-justifying end. This emphasis found expression in works of the most prominent philosophers of the age. There is no real precedent for that work of Bacon's imagination, *The New Atlantis*, with its scientific institute for multiplying useful commodities and for diminishing the incidence of disease. Bacon foresaw to a greater degree than any previous writer, the possibilities which men were acquiring for the conquest of nature.[1] Descartes, who was much younger, wrote with equal enthusiasm and more precision of these possibilities in his *Discours de la Méthode*, which was published in 1637. He speaks of prolonging human life and diminishing human labour in the mass. Such thinking, combined with the new technical needs brought about by the novel industrial development that was taking place in Great Britain, Sweden and to some extent in Holland, gave a new turn to inventive ingenuity.

The actual saving of labour in industrial processes effected during the lives of Shakespeare and Rembrandt was not spectacular. But it was more impressive than most historical students suppose.[2] This was a highly inventive age in a variety of ways. In the north of Europe, or at any rate in Great Britain, inventive ingenuity was devoted mainly to reductions in the costs of production and of the transportation of bulky, cheap commodities.[3] It was at this time that men began to

---

[1] Dr Hall, in demonstrating that Bacon had 'a philosophic appreciation of the value of knowledge for its own sake', is inclined to deny novelty to Bacon's interest in the use of knowledge for improving material welfare (*The Scientific Revolution*, pp. 164–5). I am unable to judge because Dr Hall gives no details concerning the medieval precedent that he has in mind.

[2] Georg Wiebe, *Zur Geschichte der Preisrevolution des 16. und 17. Jahrhunderts* (Leipzig, 1895), pp. 237–43. Nef, 'Prices and industrial capitalism in France and England, 1540–1640', *Economic History Review*, VII, no. 2 (1937), 174, 184.

[3] Nef, 'The progress of technology and the growth of large-scale industry in Great Britain, 1540–1640', *Economic History Review*, V, no. 1 (1934), 9–18.

attach a *value* that was novel to inventive ideas whose only purpose was to reduce labour costs and to multiply production. This shift in values was at the root of the major inventions which much later brought about the industrial revolution.

How far were men free agents in these matters? Was it not simply the existence in Great Britain of rich coal seams and of iron ores which lent themselves with facility to the manufacture of cast and pig iron that brought about the new ways of thinking? These resources had always been there. The question is why they began to be exploited in novel ways at this particular period in history. The rapid rise in prices, which was common to the whole of Europe in this age, was accompanied for a time by a lag in wage rates. This was apparently the case in England during the fifteen-forties and fifties, and there was in consequence at that time a new stimulus to the investment of capital in industrial enterprise. The break with Rome, the dissolution of the monasteries, the growing power of a representative assembly—the House of Commons—all these changes stimulated *private* enterprise throughout the period from about 1540 to 1640. A large number of factors began to interact upon each other to make the fifty years preceding the Civil War perhaps the most prosperous period England had hitherto experienced.

However propitious for private investment were the institutional changes of the period in English history from the Reformation to the Civil War, a quantitative economy could hardly have gained the prominence it did without an intensification of quantitative ideas and quantitative values. We know that this quantitative-mindedness was not in any special sense British; it was Pan-European. It was manifested in Italy and in France as much as in England. That makes it impossible to treat this new turn of the mind as an example of geographical or economic determinism, a result simply of the novel exploitation of coal and iron ore or of the novel ecclesiastical and constitutional changes which were taking place in the north of Europe. It is much more likely that the greatly increased importance given to quantitative values, which was so impressive a feature of European history after about 1570, was itself an important independent force in bringing about the early English industrial revolution.

5. TOWARDS THE REINFORCEMENT OF TECHNOLOGY BY SCIENCE

If we are searching for the origins of industrialism, we must recognize that much more was needed for its eventual triumph than a change in tastes in the direction of quantitative production, and a change in the major technical problems which men aimed to solve. That was already clear to the most penetrating minds of the early seventeenth century. Francis Bacon and Descartes looked, each in a different way, not to technology but to the natural sciences as the disciplines capable of lengthening lives, lightening labour and multiplying output. In its early phases, the industrial development of the late eighteenth and nineteenth centuries might have occurred without the scientific revolution. But it could not have gone far.

The new search for truth concerning the physical universe and the nature of the organic matter of which the human body is composed, made possible the extraordinary power and speed of production, of transportation and of communications, together with the extraordinary increase in the duration of human life, which began in Europe and North America, and which spread to the entire world in the twentieth century. Since at least as early as the times of Réaumur (1683–1757),[1] the source of those realizations in applied science and technology, destined to transform the conditions of living, is found increasingly in new discoveries in the natural sciences. Before the end of the eighteenth century, and more and more as we enter the nineteenth, the simple empirical search for technical improvements to cheapen the costs of production, proved inadequate to solve

[1] *Réaumur's Memoirs on Steel and Iron*, ed. Cyril Stanley Smith, Chicago, 1956. Cp. Nef, *War and Human Progress*, pp. 194 ff.

the technical problems which had to be surmounted to give
us the modern mechanized world and bring us to the threshold
of the electronic age. More and more results depended upon
the application of the new scientific knowledge (resulting from
the scientific revolution) to practical ends. As Dr Charles
Singer has written,

> A series of men in England and France, Lavoisier, Watt, Fourcroy,
> Black, Leblanc, Chaptal, Davy, Faraday, and others of that type,
> by precept or by example, convinced a substantial body of Western
> manufacturers and statesmen that the way of advance for industry
> was along the scientific route. This rapidly proved true, and es-
> pecially for the use of power derived from changes in the state of
> matter....For about a century and a half now technology has been
> generally treated as applied science.[1]

As suggested in the first chapter, the crucial innovations
in speculation, the turn to methods of scientific inquiry which
still prevail, and which made possible the technological revolutions of the nineteenth and twentieth centuries, occurred during
the period from about 1570 to 1660. The movements of the
human mind in that earlier age were an indispensable preparation for those scientific discoveries which have led to the
mechanization of work, of transport and of communication
since 1800. Stimulated by the discovery and application of
new sources of energy—oil, hydroelectric and eventually
atomic power—industrialism has spread to the continent of
Europe, to America and finally to all parts of the world during
the last 150 years.

If we examine the background of the intellectual revolution
that is responsible for the industrial world in which we live
today, we find little to support the view that modern science
resulted from industrial progress in the north of Europe
between the Reformation and the Civil War. During these
times of decisive change in rational procedures it was the
mind itself, not economic institutions nor economic develop-

[1] Singer, *Technology and History* (London, 1952), p. 6.

ment, which called the new tunes and composed most of the variations which the greatest scientists were playing on them. The revolutionary scientific discoveries of Gilbert, Harvey, Galileo and Kepler, like the new mathematics of Descartes, Desargues, Fermat and Pascal, were of no immediate practical use. Freedom, rather than necessity, was the principal power behind the scientific revolution.[1]

That revolution involved eventually a break with past human experience much more momentous than the concurrent early industrial revolution. Though the causes for the two revolutions were distinct, both were built on common human ground. It was the same two or three generations of men and women in Europe who participated in both: it was a few among them who brought both about.

The early industrial revolution combined with the intellectual revolution to make the times of Shakespeare and Milton in England, Cervantes and Rubens on the Continent, the critical epoch when we seek for the genesis of industrialism. It was not mainly any material developments that brought the Europeans potentially so much nearer to industrialism in the mid-seventeenth century than they had been a hundred years before. It was rather the commitment of the human mind to quantitative values and quantitative methods of reasoning, to tangible, verifiable evidence as the basis for scientific knowledge, and to a more comprehensive mathematics. These developments all had their source in the human spirit which is the instrument that enables man to rise above time, place and circumstance, and to influence the long run course of history.

[1] Nef, 'The Genesis of industrialism and of modern science', *Essays in Honor of Conyers Read*, ed. Norton Downs (Chicago, 1953), pp. 258–63.

III

THE ORIGIN OF CIVILIZATION

I. THE LIMITS OF NATURAL SCIENCE

The limits of modern science, as an instrument for helping man to understand himself, have been stated in recent years most effectively by a number of the greatest modern scientists. The rational processes which emerged from the orientation of scientific inquiry and speculation during the times of Galileo, Kepler, Harvey, Descartes and Pascal, can give us perhaps all the provable truths that we can have concerning the physical and the biological universe. They tell us little that helps us with the problems of the mysterious human person that each of us is. On that at least five of the most eminent scientists of our times who have addressed themselves to this matter— Whitehead, Sherrington, Whittaker, Hubble and Schrödinger —are agreed.[1]

Schrödinger seems to be speaking for them all in his recent book, *Nature and the Greeks.*[2]

Science [he writes] represents the level best we have been able to ascertain in the way of safe and incontrovertible knowledge...[Yet] I am...astonished that the scientific picture of the real world around me is very deficient....It is ghastly silent about all and sundry that is really near to our heart, that really matters to us....It knows nothing of God and Eternity, good or bad, beautiful and ugly.[3] Science sometimes pretends to answer questions in these domains, but the answers are very often so silly that we are not inclined to take them seriously.

[1] The same point has been made of late by historians of science. See, for example, Alexandre Koyré's 'The significance of the Newtonian Synthesis', in *Archives Internationales d'Histoire des Sciences* (U.N.E.S.C.O.), p. 23.
[2] Edwin Schrödinger, *Nature and the Greeks* (Cambridge, 1954), pp. 93–6.
[3] I have purposely transposed some of the words in quoting this sentence.

So, in brief, we do not belong to this material world that science constructs for us. We are not in it....We believe that we are in it...[because]...our bodies belong to [it]....

And the reason for this disconcerting situation is...that, for the purpose of constructing the picture of the external world, we have used the greatly simplifying device of cutting our own personality out, removing it; hence it is gone, it has evaporated, it is ostensibly not needed.

Without that human person, whose inner and intimate life modern science is powerless to help, there would have been none of the speculations concerning the physical and biological universe which, by the practical applications made of them, have had such an important part in building the industrialized world we live in. But would it have been enough to produce that world if the only progress had been scientific and the only effective inventions technological? Did not the triumph of industrialism depend also on new commitments of the heart and the imagination, which lessened the violence among men and among societies of men?

The Wars of Religion in France and the Low Countries were followed by the Thirty Years War. That was as gruesome and total a conflict, at any rate in central Europe, as the European peoples experienced between the eleventh and the twentieth centuries. At first sight, then, it might appear that war was a stimulus to the genesis of industrialism, or at least that war did nothing to interfere with the progress made in men's minds and in their economic life in the direction of the modern economic world. But has not war been 'less a cause for industrialism...than its shadow and its nemesis'? The exceptional prosperity which lasted in Great Britain for several decades preceding the Civil War, is explained partly by the fact that for some eighty years, from about 1560 to 1640, England and Scotland were at peace within themselves, while there was no prolonged fighting by English forces at sea or on the Continent. For a period of three generations, England was in fact the 'fortress...against infection and the hand of war' that Shakespeare had old John of Gaunt describe. England was also, unlike the countries of Europe, an area of free trade. Peace, combined with the absence of local tolls and duties, gave the people of Great Britain a remarkable opportunity to develop economically along lines of their own.

The frightful wars on the Continent were not in the main a stimulus to creative thought in connexion with the natural sciences. It was in spite of them, rather than because of them, that Galileo, Kepler, Descartes, Fermat and Pascal were able to change the methods of scientific inquiry in ways destined to transform man's knowledge of nature and nature's laws.[1]

With the growing powers which men have obtained since the sixteenth century over nature, in the interest of lower costs of production and of increased output, the need for restraints on war increased. The eventual triumph of industrialism required a much larger stage than the island of Great Britain. To what extent were the elements in humane relations among men and nations, which were needed for that triumph, already present at the time when the religious wars began— in the mid-sixteenth century? To what extent were they the result of novel efforts made by our ancestors since that time? These questions lead us to inquire into the causes of war and the nature of efforts to prevent or to limit it before the age of religious wars.

At no time in the annals of the human race can these causes be readily reduced to one, save in so far as all war and violence can be plausibly represented as a result of the fall of man. Wars are brought about, alas, by that human personality which the scientist can neither explain nor control. Evil is ever present in our nature. However little the Biblical story of Adam and Eve in the garden of Eden is now accepted, we have to admit, to whatever race or nation or creed we belong, that we have met few men or even women who exemplify perfectly the Christian precept to love one's neighbour as

[1] Nef, *War and Human Progress* (London, 1951), ch. III and part I generally; see also A. R. Hall, *Ballistics in the Seventeenth Century* (Cambridge, 1952), p. 165.

oneself. At least it will be granted that the man who has always loved in that way, even his enemies, is a most uncommon fellow.

My mind goes back to a rainy afternoon in the summer of 1949 in a café on the main square of the town of Strasbourg in Alsace. My late wife was a person of great intensity and generosity, with an overwhelming desire to communicate her thoughts. As was not uncommon she began to talk to those about her. The theme to which she rose with passionate conviction was derived from the New Testament. 'We must love our enemies', she kept repeating. Each time that she said this an Alsatian, sitting near, would answer not unkindly and in French, but with a noticeable German accent, 'Yes... but not the Germans'.

Yet, if we are Christians, not to love our neighbours and even our enemies is to fall short of perfection. The external causes of war are innumerable. Even when we classify them according to various spheres of history as these are defined in our age of specialization—economic, religious, political—we find that the role of such factors has varied greatly from time to time.[1] The only element which persists through all times is our erring human nature. Out of the failure of human beings to achieve perfection conflicts arise among men and among societies.

2. LIMITATIONS ON VIOLENCE BEFORE MODERN TIMES

What held societies back from the total use of force for the sake of conquest until after the sixteenth century was not mainly any written or unwritten renunciation of total war as an instrument of policy, or any nice feelings about the baseness of the deliberate infliction of physical pain. It was the establishment of absolute authority by armed conquest.

[1] I have discussed this matter in a recent paper, 'Les Causes de la guerre', which is to be published by the Institut Juridique de Nice as part of the proceedings for the summer of 1956.

The immediate world, subject to conquest, *could* then be conquered, because the weapons were not powerful enough, as they have now become, to destroy a large portion of the life of this planet. The most striking example perhaps was the peace within the ancient Roman Empire. Rome attained for a period of almost three centuries virtually complete dominion over the countries of the Mediterranean basin and over Europe as far as the Rhine and the Danube. The Roman peace resulted from the principle of total conquest, implemented by a series of total victories, in which the conquered were made subject peoples. This process culminated in 146 B.C. with the Roman victory over Carthage in the third Punic War. The peace within the frontiers of the Empire was not a peace of free men. For all the laws established by the Romans, with their genius as lawmakers, it was a peace of enslaved peoples.

The spread of Christianity through Europe, which began in the era of the Roman peace, produced a new kind of unity, spiritual in origin. Until the times of the Crusades, which began at the end of the eleventh century, when the papacy was growing more powerful politically than it had ever been before, this unity was not founded on force. But it was only a partial unity. With the growth of the power of the papacy from the mid-eleventh to the thirteenth century, the Church was in a position to extend its authority in an effort to restrict armed conflicts. The canon law, elaborated during that period of great ecclesiastical strength and prestige, set limits to war by defining a just war, by prohibiting the use of certain weapons, such as the cross-bow, which Christians might legitimately use in fighting fellow Christians, and by making it illegal to wage war on certain days, in certain places, and in respect of certain persons.[1] (For instance, priests were forbidden to take part in fighting.)

These measures were not entirely ineffective. At the beginning of the nineteenth century, when many Europeans

---

[1] See for instance Gabriel Le Bras, 'Canon Law' in *The Legacy of the Middle Ages* (Oxford, 1926), p. 342.

looked back with deep distrust on the age of faith in the twelfth and thirteenth centuries, one of them, the Comte de Saint-Simon, an apostle of modern progress, wrote a pamphlet on ways of preventing a recurrence of the Napoleonic wars. He turned to medieval Europe for guidance. As long as an allegiance to the sovereign principle of religious unity and universal government through the Church subsisted, he remarked, 'there were few wars in Europe and these wars had little importance'.[1]

An impression had grown up in some quarters fifty years before the time of Saint-Simon, that the later Middle Ages were marked by a remarkable improvement among the Europeans in their personal and political relations, that men and women became much less brutal and rude. On the eve of the religious wars, from 1519 to 1555, much of Europe was under the political sovereignty of the Emperor Charles V. The Scottish historian William Robertson was among the first to attempt a general account of conditions under Charles V's rule. He wrote with enthusiasm of the 'improvement in policy and manners which the Europeans' had then attained.[2] A reader of the long introduction in which these words appear gets the impression that between the early eleventh and the early sixteenth centuries, the Europeans had taken the major steps in the advance from what Robertson calls 'barbarism' to what he calls 'refinement'.

As a stylist, Robertson remains impressive. Older than Gibbon, his polished prose, with its flowing sentences, suggests that he was one of Gibbon's masters. If Gibbon is alive in the culture of our age, while Robertson is dead, this is because the permanence of a history depends in no small measure on the adequacy of the materials that the historian uses for the purpose he sets himself. Robertson's materials appear flimsy in the light of the extraordinarily detailed re-

[1] C. H. de Saint-Simon, *De la Réorganisation de la Société Européenne*, ed. Alfred Péreire (Paris, n.d.), pp. 20-1.
[2] W. Robertson, *The History of the Reign of the Emperor Charles V*, 1, 7th ed. (London, 1792), 13-14.

search into medieval and Renaissance history that has been undertaken since his time.

How far does the new historical knowledge acquired since Robertson wrote support his thesis that Europe advanced from 'barbarism to refinement' during the five centuries preceding the Reformation? There had been, certainly, immense improvement in material wealth. Early sixteenth-century Europe—with its hundreds of towns (many dependent for economic existence on the surrounding country for distances of scores of miles), with its industrial machinery driven by horse, wind and water power, with its cathedrals and monasteries, town halls, princely palaces and mansions of the nobility and of rich merchants, with its extensive international trade in luxury wares, in wines and even in some heavy commodities such as salt and wrought iron—was a sophisticated world compared with early eleventh-century Europe. In the interval the Europeans had developed codes of law and methods of administration, both lay and ecclesiastical, accompanied by appropriate conventions and forms which facilitated political and judicial as well as economic relationships.

But had there been any notable movement towards tenderness in the ways human beings treated each other in their daily lives? Had there been any lessening of the brutal treatment of enemies and non-combatants in war? Those are not questions which Robertson attempts to answer. If he had had at his disposal the vastly increased material since made available by historical research, he could hardly have answered confidently with a glowing affirmative. By comparison with the customs familiar to us in our childhood before the First World War, the manners of our Christian ancestors in Europe in the relatively peaceful times which impressed the Comte de Saint-Simon were far from tender.

The waging of relentless war, pursued with fiendish cruelty beyond the battlefields, was never outlawed even by the medieval Church when people outside the Roman Catholic community were involved. Killing, as well as dying for Christ, and killing in most terrible ways were accepted instruments of Church policy, sanctioned by the papacy in the Crusades.

During the previous five hundred years the heathen invaders of western Europe—in the ninth and tenth centuries the Arabs, the Magyars and the Norsemen—had set sorry examples in waging war—burning peaceful villages and slaughtering women and children. It is possible therefore to represent the Europeans, in the efforts which followed to conquer the Holy Land, as having replied in what they convinced themselves, in the heat of long marches, hunger and battles, was the only language that unchristian peoples could understand. But alas for this interpretation, there seem to have been numerous occasions in which they went beyond their teachers. According to Steven Runciman, the latest thorough historian of the Crusades, the Christian armies in the Near East outdid their adversaries when it came to what we Americans and Europeans were brought up to regard as atrocities against civilians. This was true even of the first Crusade which had begun with so much genuine religious enthusiasm.[1] In the struggles that followed the Crusades in Europe itself, the same language of pitiless slaughter which, in the name of religion, had once been at least officially reserved for heathen enemies in war, was extended to persons born Christians who were judged to have strayed from orthodoxy.

The relatively peaceful conditions that impressed the Comte de Saint-Simon in thirteenth-century Europe, rested to no small degree on the immense authority and power of the medieval papacy. They rested partly on the way in which the belligerent instincts of the Europeans had been directed temporarily by the Church in the direction of the heathen inhabitants of the Near East. They did not rest on the voluntary acceptance of a principle of limited war, based on civil laws and customs. They did not rest upon tender manners,

[1] *A History of the Crusades*, I (Cambridge, 1951), 286-7.

upon the actual practice in lay life of love and charity. Although the ideals of love and charity had been given an incomparable spiritual strength by the Saviour, they had hardly passed beyond the boundaries of the city of God, partly realized long after Saint Augustine's time in the monasteries and churches. What the religious attempted to do, and could only do most imperfectly, was to shut themselves off from the temporal instincts and desires that are an integral and inevitable part of material existence in the actual world of sense experiences. Theirs was an heroic effort to redeem their fellow human beings from their sins by acts of renunciation and self-abnegation. This was something different from trying to infuse charity and love into the thoughts and actions to which natural instincts and desires give rise and so to temper the violence which human beings inflict on one another.

Once the religious unity enforced by a strong papacy was undermined—as it was already to a considerable extent in the fourteenth century, with the great schism, with the rival popes—warfare in Europe again became endemic. The ferocity of rival armies shows how thin and ineffectual under stress the rules of chivalry, which we associate with medieval knighthood, could become. Let us take almost at random a selection from Sir John Froissart's story of the Hundred Years War. He is describing the siege of Ghent carried on by an army from the adjacent county of Flanders. Ghent was one of the most advanced towns of the fourteenth century in its economic prosperity, and the whole area in which this fighting took place may almost be called, in an economic sense, the heart of medieval Europe, because it was for a time the greatest centre of the most important of medieval industries, the textile industry.

As soon as the earl [of Flanders] arrived at the square before the church, and found that the men of Ghent had retreated into it, he ordered the building to be set on fire; large quantities of straw and faggots were brought, and being placed all round the church and

73

lighted, the flames soon ascended to the roof. The destruction of the Ghent men was now inevitable; for if they stayed in the church they were sure to be burnt, and if they attempted to sally out they were as sure to be slain, and thrown back into the fire. John de Launoy, who was in the steeple, perceiving that he must soon be destroyed, for the steeple itself was beginning to take fire, cried out to those below, 'Ransom! Ransom!' and offered his coat, which was full of florins; but they only laughed at him, and said in reply, 'John, come and speak to us through the windows, and we will receive you. Make a handsome leap, John, such as you have forced our friends to take this year'. John thought for a moment, and then, preferring being slain to being burnt, leaped out of the window; however, both these disasters happened to him; for his enemies received him as he fell upon the points of their spears, and after hacking him to pieces, flung him back into the flames. Of the 6000 men—of which, to say the least, the army under Rasse de Harzelle and John de Launoy consisted—not more than 300 escaped; the rest were either slain in the field or in the town, or burnt in the church.[1]

This is hardly an inspiring example of limited warfare, or of the respect which near neighbours felt for each other as fellow Christians when they took to fighting. With many such examples before us, we are led to the conclusion that it was less the inadequacy of the will to kill, than the inadequacy of the means, with small armies and backward weapons, that prevented a widespread holocaust among the Christian peoples themselves during the later Middle Ages.

Such solidarity as existed in medieval Europe rested ultimately upon the existence of a single Church and the practice of a single worship. And, in the very age of Charles V, the age which Robertson set out to describe in his history, the idea of religious unity which the Church represented was shattered. What John Donne was to write two generations later concerning experience as a whole was true for the central part of experience which the Christian religion still occupied after the Reformation.

[1] Sir John Froissart, *The Chronicles of England, France, Spain etc.* (London n.d.), pp. 175–6.

Limitations on violence

'Tis all in peeces, all cohaerence gone;
All just supply, and all Relation....

How could the authority of the Church be invoked to limit war, when large groups of Europeans numbering millions, some sustained by powerful monarchs as in Great Britain and in Sweden, set up churches of their own in opposition to the Roman Catholic Church? For men and women with deep Christian convictions in each group, the men and women of the other groups became heretics, their leaders antichrists. The same view that had prevailed among the Crusaders in their attacks on the infidel was now applied to fellow Europeans, to members of the same nation, of the same town, even of the same family. Violence of every kind was rendered possible with the sanction of the very institution—the Church—which, in the name of the Founder, had made efforts to limit war among men.

When the religious wars broke out in full force in the fifteen-sixties, the Europeans were not equipped with means of extermination at all comparable to those at our disposal today. Yet during the previous seventy years, since the battle of Fornovo in Italy, when horse-drawn artillery was first brought into action, there had been something of a revolution in the methods of waging war. Artillery and smaller firearms had become the decisive weapons. It was much easier to kill in large numbers and at a considerable distance than it had been in the Middle Ages. The defensive strength of knights in armour had been obliterated. Again, with changes in methods in agriculture, mining and manufacturing, wealth had increased, and it was possible to put much larger armies into action—numbering 30,000 and sometimes even 50,000 men. The human target was enlarged at the same time that the effectiveness of the means of hitting it was much augmented.

When the Emperor Charles V renounced his numerous titles in 1555 and 1556 and retired to the monastery at Juste, there had not been established any general restraints on violence, either in domestic or in public relations, such as

75

existed in the Europe and the North America of our child-hood. There had been no apparent diminution in the cruelty, the messiness and the ugly violence with which, under what was regarded as provocation, men got rid of their neighbours. Unless some new ways were discovered for keeping fighting within bounds, now that both the will to fight and the means of fighting had increased in power, the elements were present for a general slaughter. Such a slaughter almost took place in Germany and the rest of central Europe during the Thirty Years War. It is estimated that about a third of the population was wiped out by warfare and its consequences in famine, exposure and massacre.

There had always been humane men like Montaigne who were shocked and saddened by the brutality of their contemporaries. There were on the eve of the Reformation men like Erasmus and Thomas More who hoped something could be done to introduce greater decency into the conduct of life, who sought a temporal world in which violence would have a less prominent place. What we miss in all these 'humanists' of the Renaissance is any sense that the deliberate infliction of bodily suffering beyond the field of battle is so grievous an abuse of power that it lies beyond the bounds of accepted conduct. What we miss in Montaigne, writing as he was in the shadow of the French religious wars, is the idea that the human conscience ought never to resign itself to the commission of 'atrocities', the idea that unrestrained violence lies beyond the bounds which a decent community, even of independent states and of different religious practices, can ever accept. The word atrocity, as a term for condemning the cruel and heinous conduct of a people, hardly seems to have existed in English before the late eighteenth century. It is this human conscience that we find expressed in Bernanos, in the shock he received from the Spanish Civil War, when he was told by some Spanish officers that it was more Christian to kill than to die for Christ.

It was after the times of Montaigne, then, that a change

occurred in the outlook of the Europeans concerning violence. The idea developed that murder and rape were evil in themselves, not simply at the Day of Judgement, but here and now in the temporal world, even when the victim is a black man, an infidel, an atheist or a heretic. That idea became almost universal during the nineteenth century, if not before, among a substantial part of the peoples who were descendants of those Europeans who were caught in the sixteenth century in the religious wars. For our grandfathers and fathers in countries such as France, Belgium, Switzerland, Great Britain, the British Dominions and the United States, the kinds of cruel physical treatment which Montaigne reported in his letter, which had been common from time immemorial, together with the cruel physical treatment of minorities, were not accepted as inevitable. Public opinion everywhere was trusted by condemning them to reduce their incidence. That is why atrocity stories made such an impression, and aroused such indignation, in France, England and the United States during the First World War. The outlook on the taking of human life had profoundly changed since the sixteenth century. In the times of Thomas More, which is to say at the Reformation, capital punishment could be inflicted in England for almost innumerable offences, including even petty theft. Only a year ago Parliament attempted to abolish the death penalty for any offence whatsoever.

The new outlook on violence, the new sense of human responsibility for decent conduct in this world, seems to be a part of the modern history of Europe. What relation had this improvement in the treatment of man by other men to the coming of industrialism? Before we consider that question, we must seek the origins of the change. We must try to determine the place of the late sixteenth and early seventeenth centuries in bringing it about.

In doing so we must not neglect the contribution of the Christian and even the pagan past, which the Europeans inherited at the time of the religious wars. Without a knowledge of the solidarity that existed and was developed among them in the Christian society of the Middle Ages, without a knowledge of the learning and the culture they derived from the ancient Greco-Roman world and the societies of the Near and even the Far East, without perhaps the influence of the relatively decent manners which seem to have prevailed in China during the Sung dynasty (960–1279), the spiritual basis of this modern humaneness is unintelligible. But we have already said something similar about modern science. It is unintelligible without the science of the Renaissance, the science of the Middle Ages, of the Arabs, and especially of the ancient Greeks, of men such as Democritus and Euclid. The history of man's search for the good and the beautiful, and of his efforts to improve human manners, since the age of the Emperor Charles V, does not account at all adequately for the coming of more humane practises concerning violence, any more than the history of thought since Gilbert and Galileo accounts at all adequately for the coming of modern science. But in these lectures we are concerned with the efforts that distinguish modern times from past ages. Were changes comparable to those which revolutionized natural science taking place in faith, in art, in laws, customs and manners, during the decades that followed the beginning of religious wars in Europe?

When we turn for guidance concerning the changes in the outlook on violence to our forebears of the eighteenth century, who tried to see history as a whole rather than as a series of disconnected specialties, we get the impression that fundamental improvements, which we miss in connexion with the Europe of Charles V, had occurred two centuries afterwards. We get the impression that a remarkable growth had taken place in the humanity men expressed and felt over killing and torture. We get the impression that the Europeans had found a new conscience before the union of coal and iron, before the union of steam power with manufactures and transport. We get the further impression that the changes in men's hearts and minds had had perhaps more tangible effects in the domestic and the political conduct of the Europeans by the mid-eighteenth century, than the development of a new technology and of new sciences had had upon their industrial life.

If the word atrocity is novel, so is the word civilization. Historical researchers, who have given the matter their attention, have not been able to trace it back beyond the mid-eighteenth century. Perhaps the first writer to use it in a published work was the marquis de Mirabeau. It occurs in his *L'Ami des Hommes ou Traité de la Population*,[1] which was published in 1757. It has been established that the word had in the beginning, and for some fifty years afterwards, a different meaning from the meanings which Gobineau, Spengler, Toynbee and others have now helped to give it. In another work of Mirabeau's, *L'Amy des Femmes ou Traité de la Civilisation*, which exists only in manuscript,[2] he tells what he meant by it.

La civilisation d'un peuple [he wrote about 1766] *est l'adoucissement de ses mœurs, l'urbanité, la politesse, et les connaissances répandues de manière que les bienséances y soient observées et y tiennent lieu de loix de détail....*[3] La civilisation ne fait rien pour la société si elle ne luy donne le fonds et la forme de la vertu. C'est du sein des sociétés adoucies par tous les ingrédients qu'on vient de citer, qu'est née la conception de l'humanité.

'Civilization' clearly included the 'refinement', whose coming Robertson identified with the later Middle Ages.[4] But it covered much more. It embraced most of those virtues which enable men to turn their passions towards humane ends which can be achieved only through gentleness. What most of the persons who first used the word seem to have

[1] E. Benveniste, 'Civilisation: Contribution à l'histoire du mot', in *Éventail de l'histoire vivante* (hommage à Lucien Febvre) (Paris, 1953), p. 48.
[2] Archives Nationales (Paris), M. 780, no. 3.
[3] The italics are Mirabeau's.
[4] See also Lucien Febvre, *Civilisation, le mot et l'idée* (Publications du Centre International de Synthèse) (Paris, 1930), pp. 8 ff.

meant by it was a combination of spiritual and moral qualities, at least partly realized in the lives of human beings in society. Among these qualities were decency, propriety, honesty and tenderness, moderation and self-control in speech, in conduct and even in thought. These ingredients, as Mirabeau suggested, gave birth to the novel concept of a universal humanity that transcends nations, races and even forms of religious worship. Europeans coined and employed a new word, because they were describing conditions in the temporal world which they believed were novel.

Whether or not they used the word 'civilization', a number of the leading minds of Europe in the times of Mirabeau, of Adam Smith, of Gibbon, and even earlier, in the times of their great predecessors, Defoe, Montesquieu and Voltaire, were convinced that the Europeans were closer to perfection than any peoples had ever been before. If they were at least partly right, and if Robertson was mistaken in supposing that the decisive steps in this improvement had been taken by the time of the Reformation, when were these steps taken and how? What bearing had the coming of 'civilization' upon the coming of industrialism?

IV

THE SPIRITUAL BASIS OF CIVILIZATION

In the times of Charles V, of Henry VIII and of François I, the lives of the Europeans, especially of that most influential minority of Europeans who lived in cities and small towns, were permeated by issues arising out of the practice of the Christian faith to a degree that it is difficult for us to grasp today. The lives of the Europeans were also permeated by issues arising out of the pursuit of delight, under the inspiration of artists of every kind from poets to architects and to craftsmen engaged in fashioning the fine wares which the economies of the Renaissance so largely served. It is therefore to inventions in the realm of faith and in the realm of art that we must look even more than to inventions in the realm of economics and the realm of science, if we are to understand better the impact of the human personality on history in the age of the religious wars.

As a recent French Protestant writer, Monsieur E. G. Léonard,[1] has rightly emphasized, the Reformation was not, at any rate in France, primarily a revolt of certain social classes —town workmen and traders in particular—undertaken for economic reasons. It can more accurately be considered as a single movement, religious in origin, and involving the whole of western Christendom, notwithstanding the divisions in the Christian faith which resulted from it. In its origins and its opening phases, the movement was inspired by the desire and the hope for Christian unity on a plane of more Christian conduct and more intense personal faith here on earth.[2]

---

[1] *Le Protestant français* (Paris, 1953), pp. 42–6, and also his contribution to the International Historical Congress held in Rome in 1955.

[2] Marcel Bataillon, *Erasme et l'Espagne* (Paris, 1937), p. 2.

During the first half of the sixteenth century the most influential voice raised on behalf of a more Christian Europe was that of Erasmus, who himself stopped short of leaving the Church of his fathers and becoming one of the Reformers. By his emphasis on the practice of the basic tenets of the Christian faith as the essential basis for the taking of any sacrament and as the only justification for ecclesiastical authority, Erasmus opened the door to a new sense of Christian responsibility for the temporal world. His relation to the integral Christian humanism that arose after, and to some extent in spite of, the Counter-Reformation as expressed in the Councils of Trent, may perhaps be compared to the relation of the discoveries of Copernicus, Vesalius and Fernel to modern science. He saw and helped to reveal the need for a fresh view of the possibilities of human nature, the need for a new discovery of Christ, somewhat as they saw the need for fresh views of the nature of the physical and the biological world. He did not find methods for making this view an effective force in history, any more than they found methods essential to the wholesale discovery of new scientific truths.

Erasmus was the leading spokesman on behalf of the early reforms sought by religious leaders who never contemplated new forms of worship or the complete abandonment of the monastic life. In his thought and his teaching he had two primary and closely related objectives. The first was to rid the Church, with its multitude of ecclesiastical foundations, of some of the vicious worldly practices that had grown up within it, practices such as the purchase of soldiers for slaughter, the sale of indulgences forgiving sins (past, present and future) the immoral conduct of nuns, monks and other priests, conduct which extended notoriously to some cardinals and popes. The second and most important was to bring the moral principles of Christianity, as demonstrated in the words and the life of the Founder, to bear on the daily life of priest and layman alike. The philosophy of Christ ought to be lived, not argued over.[1]

[1] *Ibid.*, pp. 80-1.

The waning of medieval reality

Both purposes were assuming a greater importance than they had previously possessed, partly because of the changing nature of reality as it appeared to the Europeans. The Christians of eleventh- and early twelfth-century Europe, in the times of the great spread of monasticism, of the Norman conquest of England and of the first Crusade, tended to see the temporal world as reflected in the mysterious inner life to which men, by virtue of their minds and souls, have access. Since at least the times of Democritus and Plato, during the fifth and early fourth centuries B.C., the soul had occupied a prominent place in the speculations of philosophers, including those who gave special attention to the physical world. In the thought of most of the scholastic philosophers in the twelfth and thirteenth centuries, the soul acquired (either directly after death or at the Day of Judgement) a new body as part of the eternal order. The question of how the soul was joined by a new body (and whether this new body bore any relation to the old) was obviously not a 'clear and distinct idea' in the meaning which the Cartesians later gave to that phrase! It was a mystery. But mystery was then more a part of *reality*, and clear and distinct ideas, together with all tangible things, were then more *appearance* than they were soon to become. Therefore it was less difficult than later on to find an affinity between the two bodies—the temporal and heavenly bodies, both illuminated by the same soul. (The body here was a kind of anticipation of what the body might be there.) As a very large role was assigned to the soul in the creation of human personality, it was comparatively easy to think of the new eternal person as resembling the person who had existed here below, delivered from all the fetters of matter, space and time as we know them.

The reality most vital to the man of faith in that age of great Christian ardour, the eleventh and twelfth centuries in Europe, was the reality to which we have dim and most

6-2

imperfect access by means of the intuitive imagination without which the intellect is impotent in any creative sense. Intellect, imaginative faculties, soul have no permanent abiding place in our earthly bodies. These immaterial parts of us are conceived of as imperishable. They subject us to a hazard and offer us a hope by comparison with which all temporal hazards and hopes are likely to seem trivial. And the more we attach reality to the Eternity to which these immaterial attributes give us access, the less *real* material experiences are likely to become. Or rather we should say perhaps the more likely we are to attach different meanings to material experiences from those imposed upon us by the notion that everything ends with death.

In the times of Romanesque and early Gothic art, the objects that exist in the temporal world, including plants and animals and even human beings in the flesh, were seen filtered through minds full of belief in the reality of the unseen. Learned men were concerned primarily with what Hooker called truths about things that are and are not sensible, truths which can be grasped only by means of a knowledge of the supernatural. The medieval intellect troubled relatively little over those aspects of our experience, the tangible aspects, which, through the growing treatment of all subjects by methods derived from the natural sciences, have now acquired almost exclusive rational validity among men who profess to be learned.

It follows that for the medieval mind reality was mainly in that realm of human experience which, as Schrödinger suggests, modern science has cut out of its scheme of inquiry. It follows also that for the medieval mind the realm of human experience which has now long concerned modern science, the only reality which is ordinarily regarded by modern scholarship as a legitimate realm of learned inquiry, was mainly *appearance*.

We now have civilization behind us. Our problem is to renew it and go beyond it. For Europeans of the times of

Anselm, Abélard and Héloïse, Bernard of Clairvaux, civilization was not yet born. So it was perhaps not unnatural that the medieval view of reality encouraged men, even saintly men, to resign themselves to the faults and brutalities of the temporal world. They could do so without great suffering when the reality which now predominates was made to appear relatively trivial. They were inclined to concentrate their religious efforts on life within the cloister and on what we should now call the external sides of religious worship, the sacraments. These seemed to provide a key to the timeless unchanging reality of the world to come.

We can trace far back into European history, certainly to the thirteenth if not to the late twelfth century, a movement in art away from this abstract, mysterious and unreal world as seen through the eyes of modern science, in the direction of what was to become for modern science (at least until very recently) the only certain reality. This movement towards what we may perhaps call modern reality became more striking in the late fourteenth, fifteenth and sixteenth centuries. The new architecture and art, born in Italy with Brunelleschi and Ghiberti, was anything but literal or photographic. But it drew its inspiration more directly from nature than Romanesque and Gothic art, from the plants, the animals, the mountains, the skies, as we see them, and the human body as we see it. So it was less spiritual, less mystical, than Gothic art or Romanesque art. As men concentrated their human faculties more on objects directly accessible to the senses, as they gave increasing priority to those tangible realities which fall within the scope of modern scientific investigation, it became more difficult to interpret the text of the Bible as in accord with the actual practices of the Church in the sacraments. It became more difficult to believe in transubstantiation. Thus we find Zwingli asking Luther how Christ can be really present in the mass when the Bible tells us that he is sitting on the right hand of God.

It was partly this changing view of reality that led Erasmus and some of his contemporaries to try to reform the ancient Church, to lay less emphasis on life within the cloister and more on religious life beyond it in the temporal world. Perhaps his truest disciple among the early Protestants was Zwingli. In 1515, when hardly thirty, Zwingli wrote a letter from Glarus to Erasmus.

I think [he said] that I have made a great name for myself and make it my boast in nothing else than this, that I have seen Erasmus —the man who has deserved most highly of letters and the secret things of Sacred Scripture, and who so burns with love of God that he thinks that whatever is done for the cause of good letters is done for himself.

It is in the leadership of Zwingli, born in 1484 two months after Martin Luther, that we have the most serious early Protestant promise of a possible union of the intense religious feeling, which the Reformation expressed, with a new sense of Christian love, tenderness and charity in the actual lives which human beings lived in the temporal world.

The doctrines of Zwingli, as these are revealed in the written work he left and in the accounts of his words and actions recorded by his contemporaries, appealed to men to seek the Kingdom of God, to seek salvation in Christ, partly by means of a greater fulfilment of natural instincts. The pleasures that were being cultivated during Zwingli's lifetime, as a part of the increasing material prosperity that prevailed in most parts of the Continent, were not seen, through his religious eyes, as fundamentally evil. The new delight in natural beauty and in the fashioning of beautiful objects of all kinds was, for him, part of God's design for the soul's salvation. If Protestantism had developed mainly under his influence, would it have emphasized to the same degree as it has the harsh, ascetic and gloomy sides of human nature? Zwingli's modern admirers have thought not.

2. THE REFORMATION AND RELIGIOUS ASCETICISM

Whether or not they are right, Zwingli's teaching had little influence in forming the religious outlook and practices of the early Protestants. In so far as the more successful forms of early Protestantism were concerned—the Church of England, the Lutheran and the Calvinist Churches—it was the negative sides of virtue that were brought into the foreground, a harsh and puritanical treatment of issues pertaining to the human body. For Luther man was almost utterly depraved; it was only God's grace which could lift him up. Calvin's insistence on the doctrine of predestination, in a form more rigid and pitiless than that of Augustine, left the very great majority of all human beings condemned to eternal damnation whatever they did. Among the first two generations of reformers there was hardly any effort to diffuse charity and compassion into the daily lives of the faithful. Early Protestantism did little or nothing to inspire increased tenderness among men or greater refinements in manners.

The gulf between Protestantism and Catholicism during much of the sixteenth century was not over the nature and extent of human depravity; it was over the problem of redemption. For most early Protestants it rested with the individual to save himself, and even there he could do little unless God had selected him for salvation. In England and Scotland especially, the religious exercises of the followers of Calvin were mostly limited to meditation over one's sins, daily prayers, reading the Bible, rigid Sunday observances. But with reformed Catholicism, the hopes of redemption for many rested in no small measure upon the mystical union of a few with God, such as could be obtained only by retirement from the world. With the early Protestants, it was God, by His grace or His predestination, that overcame human depravity. With the reformed Catholics, or perhaps we had better say with the reformed Catholic mystics, it was atonement in the cloister for the sins of the world.

One of the major developments of the sixteenth and seventeenth centuries was the renewal and extension of this Christian practise of self-purification in the rigid seclusion of the cloister, where a passionate mystical love of God was combined with most of the harder aspects of medieval monasticism. The great leaders in this movement were the Spanish mystics, Saint Theresa (1515–82) and Saint John of the Cross (1542–91). Early in life Saint Theresa joined the Carmelites, founded as an order of nuns by Jean Soreth a century earlier, in 1451. She was soon disappointed by the slackness of the discipline, in which she thought that she had found the cause of what was for her the catastrophe of the Reformation. She set out to restore the ancient discipline of the older Carmelite friaries in all its rigour. In 1562 she founded a house in which the religious were strictly confined to the cloister and in which they lived on alms without any regular endowment. As a result of her efforts, and still more of those of Saint John of the Cross, many cloisters of the kind she advocated—friaries as well as nunneries—were established by the Carmelites in Spain. Some religious men and women were taking their faith with a passion for self-purification that rivalled that of the eleventh and early twelfth centuries' monastic leaders, of whom Bernard of Clairvaux offers one of the most perfect examples.

This movement was, and has been ever since, an important element in the Roman Catholicism that emerged from the Counter-Reformation. It spread to France, especially during the seventeenth century. There, first with the Jansenists and later and more intensively with the Trappists, the most austere forms of cloistered life were fostered. The Abbaye de la Trappe, in Normandy, had a history reaching back to the twelfth century. But at la Trappe, as in the Carmelite houses of Spain, discipline had become very slack by the time of the Reformation. The French *chanoine*, Le Bouthillier de Rancé, who had long lived a life of dissipation, renounced all his worldly projects and established in 1657 the original rule of the order in all its harshness. A study made of the lives of the Trappists in the late seventeenth century has shown how the practice of this austerity was related to the very high death rate among the monks (especially from tuberculosis).

Whatever the value of the religious inspiration aroused by the revival of the severest medieval discipline, it did nothing to mitigate violence and violent manners in the temporal world. (It was in itself a form of violence, a violent revolt against sin.) Here it went beyond even the austerity and pessimism of the Puritans. Saint Theresa is said to have worn a particularly painful haircloth and to have scourged herself habitually. Even when there was no overt artificially inflicted physical suffering, the nature of the abstinence, the lack of adequate food, the lack of all comforts for sleep, the incredibly harsh hours, made the life anything but an example to stimulate the laity to sublimate their violent impulses and to control their passions with kindliness.

Both the Puritan and the mystical concepts involved a violent wrenching of the physical sides of our nature. The Puritan concept extended religiously inspired abstinence and activity to the world, the mystical concept renewed it in the cloister. Both, if unmitigated, if pursued relentlessly, tended in the direction of harshness, the fostering of artificial penance as the price of redemption.

Christianity from the beginning contained, in the person of the Saviour, as His life and teaching have been brought to us in the revelations of the New Testament, a peculiarly generous concept of charity, of the opportunity we have to give ourselves to others here and now, in so far as we love our neighbours for God. Charity, as the scholastic philosophers had emphasized, is of all the temporal virtues the one which is the same here as in eternity. So it unites us to God as no other virtue does.

The formula—*fides charitate formata*, faith is formed by charity, a formula familiar to the scholastics—appears in Rabelais, when Gargantua instructs his son to serve, love and fear God, and 'par foy formée de charité, estre à lui adjoint en sorte que jamais n'en sois désamparé par péché'. Such a formula was reversed both in Lutheran and in Calvinist doctrine, as it was being expressed at about the same time, during the second quarter of the sixteenth century. In the *Institutes*, Calvin repudiated it more than once, in one place as a 'sophist lie'. He wrote of the sophists: '...ils imaginent que la Foi soit formée, quand à la connaissance de Dieu est ajoutée une bonne affection....'[1] Here it might seem that Roman Catholic doctrine was more humanistic than Protestant doctrine as it was forming. There are senses in which this was true. But it must not be supposed that the concept of the priority of charity, derived from the past and expressed by Rabelais, was of a virtue that grows and flowers among human beings primarily in their personal relations with one another. As developed first in the spirit of the Counter-Reformation, the practice of charity was a kind of sacrifice: the charity felt for others was expressed in the love of God for Himself, not in the love of the neighbour for God in a personal individual sense.

Life in the cloister, as developed anew in the late sixteenth century under the leadership of the Spanish mystics, was conceived to be the pre-eminent demonstration of charity. It is a mistake to think of these mystics as seeking solely or even mainly their own salvation. On the contrary, total dedication to the monastic life was the supreme example of love of the neighbour. It was the sins of others, the sins of the world, even more than their own, for which the ascetic monk and nun atoned. For Saint Theresa, the suffering she and the Carmelites underwent was the sure means of bringing back millions of souls alienated from God and condemned, in consequence, to eternal damnation. What greater proof *could* she offer of her love of the neighbour?

Without knowing much more about the relations between priests and communicants during the first sixteen centuries of Christianity, and especially from the eleventh to the sixteenth century in Europe, I feel much hesitancy in expressing the view that little had been done to exploit the resources of

[1] Lucien Febvre, *Le Problème de l'incroyance au XVIe siècle*, pp. 303-4.

compassion and tenderness which the Christian message contains in connexion with daily life in the temporal world. The impression left on me by my most inadequate reading of the biographies of medieval men and women is that the possibilities of reconciling human with divine love, human with divine happiness, had been most incompletely understood. Certainly they had been incompletely understood in relation to the changing concepts of reality that developed in the later Middle Ages, and to the new world of industrialism, whose immediate origins we have found in the movements of the mind at the end of the sixteenth and during the early seventeenth century. To say this is not to forget what is perhaps the greatest of all examples of human love, the love of Héloïse for Abélard. However we interpret that episode, it was not one in which two lovers found in this world even a partial religious solution for their ecstasy and their torment.

3. THE INFUSION OF CHARITY INTO MODERN REALITY

The great inventive achievement in connexion with the Christian religion at the close of the sixteenth century and during the first half of the seventeenth, consisted in combining the ardour of religious sentiment and the determination to bring the practice of the Christian morality into the temporal world with the spread of a new tenderness and a new gentleness in human relations. All the elements were old. They were present from the beginning in the Christian faith, and to some extent before that in the Jewish faith. The invention consisted in establishing humane methods with a definitive charm and mastery.[1] Erasmus was in a sense the father of the new movement; his was a plea to priests and to all men to infuse the message of Christ into the lives led in the temporal world. But his was not, as with the leaders of the early seventeenth century, a tangible and effective effort to use

[1] Abbé Jacques Leclercq, *St François de Sales* (Paris, 1928), p. 111.

the Christian faith to instil charity and compassion into the world in the interest of virtue and justice.

The first great innovations were inspired by French Catholic priests. But their debt to the Reformation and to Protestantism was considerable. François de Sales, whose life played a part of capital importance as a creative force in the renewal of Christianity, had in his possession as a young man the heretical book of an obscure Protestant, first published in 1587. It was written by the Sieur de Lespine. It was soon translated into English,[1] with a view to offering people in the island kingdom some precious French wares. What wares did the *Excellent discours sur le repos et le contentement d'esprit* offer?

The book is an attack on all the older philosophies and systems of ethics for having failed to recognize the remedies offered by the Evangel, by not having founded their morality on the faith of Christ in the perfectibility of man. What Lespine sought was an ethic that would be nourished by the presence in the world of Christ Himself.

At the very time when Lespine's book appeared, a controversy was being waged over the most desirable means of rooting out the Protestant heresies from France. A group of Roman Catholics, who called themselves *English* Catholics, circulated a pamphlet in France in 1590, after nearly three decades of religious civil war. They said there is only one sound reformation for the troubles. It is to strangle heresy, to root it out by unstinted force from every town, village and hamlet. They represent this matter as one of capital importance, not only for Europe, 'dont la France est le petit œil', but also for the salvation 'de toute la chrétienté'.[2]

Appeals of this kind did not go unanswered. One answer, apparently to another such appeal, had already come in 1587 from a man who described himself as a real Catholic (and

---

[1] *A very excellent and learned discourse, touching the tranquilitie and contentation of the minde*, translated into English by Ed. Smith (Cambridge, 1592).

[2] *Premier et Second Avertissement des Catholiques Anglais aux François Catholiques et à la Noblesse qui suit à présent le Roy de Navarre* (Paris, 1590) (Newberry Library, Chicago, C. 204), I, 2; II, 19.

good Frenchman). He pointed out the advantages which England was deriving from the peaceful conditions that had been purchased at the expense of a partial toleration of the Catholic 'heresy'. It is not improbable that this pamphlet was inspired, if indeed it was not written, by Duplessis-Mornay (1549–1623). He was the chief Protestant adviser of the future French king, Henry of Navarre, and he was often called in France 'the pope of the Huguenots'. It will be remembered that Henry of Navarre himself was a Protestant before he acquired the French crown. According to Victor Hugo, he coupled himself with the first Elizabeth as an adept in politics by remarking: 'elle est vierge comme je suis catholique'. So it is not improbable that the Catholicism of the French Catholics was a disguise and that the answer to the plea for unstinted violence came mainly from Huguenot sources.

'Peace has prevailed in your kingdom,' this French *Catholic* tells his *English* brethren, 'since the accession of a Queen [Elizabeth I] who does not share our religion.' Your policy for France of strangling heresy by force can lead only to war. War is a double-edged sword. It may not turn to the advantage of those who unsheathe it. In any case whatever the outcome, war is evil in itself.

[It] is the mother of all the vices, and civil war especially, if it continues, is a mortal illness in the bowels of the State....In short, war cannot be the means of establishing a single religious faith in our kingdom; it is rather the means of insuring that there shall be neither faith nor conscience.

'True religious zeal is always softened by an instinct of charity, a virtue which no one can discover in you.... You seem to relate all Christian piety to external things, as if there could be no true religion without the ceremonies of our Church.' The best means of restoring Roman Catholicism as the one religion in France is by good example in conduct, by brotherly exhortation to the Protestants, 'by patient instruction...and by the gradual amendment of the lives which

93

Catholics lead....All this will take time, it cannot be done immediately and with violence.'[1]

It was mainly by bringing the virtues—first and foremost among them charity and compassion, and the tenderness which is the tangible expression of both—into the temporal world that some Europeans rediscovered Christ. By so doing they infused into the Christian faith a new strength during the same stretch of years when industrialism was generating in the minds of men, with their emphasis on quantitative values and on new scientific methods. The first tangible demonstrations of the new dimension which was being given to religious belief are personified in the work of François de Sales and Vincent de Paul.

The origins of these two men illustrate the universality of the movement they embodied. Their saintliness appears as a natural outgrowth of characters quietly oriented almost from the beginning of their lives in the direction of persistent and profound religious reform. Neither of them was confronted with a terrific struggle after adolescence to separate himself physically from evil and from the world. Both demonstrated great physical courage, but each achieved an almost complete otherworldliness while living almost entirely in the world. This was necessary for the achievement of the novel mission both of them served.

François de Sales was a Savoyard, born in 1567. Vincent de Paul was born nine years later at Poüy, near Dax, in southwestern France. They came from the most different social strata: François de Sales from the nobility, Vincent de Paul from the peasantry. The common elements in the movements that developed around each of them, and the close community of aims and experiences which came to exist between them as men and priests, show how in a spiritual and ethical sense France and even Europe as a whole was becoming one in its ideals. This is the more remarkable in view of the religious

---

[1] *Response à un Ligueur masqué du nom de catholique anglois, par un vray Catholique bon François* (1587) (Newberry Library, Chicago, F. 39193. 636), pp. 5-7, 130-2.

division and the wide gulf between classes. The efforts of these French priests transcended these cleavages. As bishop of Geneva, François de Sales is said to have had in his possession sixty-three heretical books. Among them was the *Excellent discours* of Jean de Lespine. Much of François de Sales' teaching and action seems, as we look back, to aim at the realization of the precepts of that pioneering Protestant work, which one of François de Sales' biographers represents as 'le premier modèle et le premier exemple d'une morale qui vivrait du sentiment religieux'.[1]

Nowhere perhaps was that gulf between classes wider than in France, the country in which the new religious inspiration seems to have originated. In France there was a separation economically into what the modern economist calls non-competing groups, with the peasants wanting mainly different commodities from the nobles, and making economic contributions of different kinds. What happened in spite of all this is a demonstration that the power of ideals and of the heart can be greater than the power of institutions.

What did François de Sales stand for? What did he accomplish?

Without a repudiation of the worship of relics and the practise of penitence, even of the mortification of the flesh, he left these methods of giving body to faith almost entirely to others. He did not feel called upon to deny anything that had sanction within the Roman Church. But he infused something into it that had not been there before, or at least that had not been there to the same extent. He sought to use the Christian faith as a means of healing, or at least of making supportable, the miseries of this world, which afflict us all, the rich and the well-born no less than the poor and the obscure. The foundations which he helped to lay for a fresh Christian culture were created mainly by two books, the *Introduction to the Devout Life* and the *Treatise on the Love of God*, and by his institution of a new order, open to women, the Visitandines.

[1] Fortunat Strowski, *St François de Sales* (Paris, 1898), p. 60.

Spiritual Basis of Civilization

The *Introduction to the Devout Life* was first published in 1608. It was addressed to everyone of whatever class, sex or age. It was directed to each person in his private domestic capacity: to father, mother, husband, wife, brother, sister, son or daughter. François de Sales wrote almost as if he were speaking to each of these persons, in turn, as an individual and in private. The appeal was to their intimate experiences, with an emphasis upon the power of the soul, through prayer and devotion, to participate in and perfect every experience of daily life. It is only a few exceptional persons, François de Sales suggested, who do not suffer enough in daily life, and who need, for their love of God, to demonstrate their devotion by special acts of renunciation and by the artificial self-infliction of pain, be it mental or physical.[1]

A person living in society [he suggested] meets with a thousand troubles every hour of the day; a husband lacking in manners, disobedient children, domestic worries, ill health, unpleasant social relations. Artificial mortifications, deliberately self-inflicted have, it follows, much less importance than the vexations of each moment.[2]

Each of us is summoned to saintliness. But for most of us the summons is not to flee in disgust from the sins and evils that surround us; it is to make a fortress, a cloister of our inner life, and to meet these sins and evils there, as they present themselves. Even though this may not involve physical suffering and deprivation, if we seek perfection it involves us in greater difficulties than does retirement from the world. 'Saint François de Sales,' wrote his most distinguished biographer, 'arrache la dévotion aux cloîtres pour la rendre civile et mondaine.'[3] We need health and modest comfort to strengthen us in a contest that will make greater demands on our integrity and our courage than life in a monastery. There the physical suffering is great, but the discipline is clearly fixed by the rules of the order. Here in the world the rules which

[1] See Leclercq, *St François de Sales*, pp. 68–9.
[2] Leclercq, *op. cit.* p. 103; see also p. 105.
[3] Strowski, *op. cit.* p. 267.

we need to guide our inner lives, which we have to translate
into action, are so many and so complicated that we can only
act on the basis of nimble discernment (of the *esprit de
finesse*) as Pascal explained with such clarity in *Les Pensées*.

The world of the cloister resembled in a curious way the
artificial world upon which the scientists were beginning to
concentrate their minds in the times of François de Sales and
Pascal. Both the cloister and the new world which science
was starting to construct were outside the human conflict,
au-dessus de la mêlée. Both left the *human* being out, treating
the body not as an essence illuminated by the spirit which
survives it, but as an object to be mortified or examined and
analysed.

The problems of living the good life in the world cannot
be solved either by applying the principles of church organization or the principles of natural science. Therefore, life in
the world involves us above all in the difficulties of making
choices, of exercising our free will. But is not this freedom
the glory of the Christian faith as Christ offers it to each of us?

In his *Introduction à la vie dévote*, then, François de Sales
summons us to participate in the human conflict with new
armour, spiritual armour, the armour that Christ wore and
that He gave us. With François de Sales, the Christian faith
and the effort to lead a Christian life were inseparable. Both
require an effort of the will in overcoming what appear to be
our natural human instincts. But this effort is the key to a
joy that is unequalled in human experience outside the faith.
Once the effort is made and repeated, each of our attempts at
perfection in daily life, by acts of devotion, by prayer, can be
rendered happy. Under the influence of prayer we can in
this way relate our devotion to God to our devotion for our
neighbour. This fills our days, in spite of suffering and sorrow,
with sweet delights, in the sense that something of the eternal
is working within us, uniting us with those we love in bonds
which death cannot sever. We are fortified to meet disaster,
but not by denying the existence of tragedy, not by cultivating

the illusion, of which Americans are fond, that the noblest conduct ought necessarily to be the easiest. We are fortified to meet disaster by drawing on the spiritual resources of our nature to shoulder a loss, when it is inevitable, as part of the Cross that Christ teaches us to bear.

In his book François de Sales draws comparisons borrowed from a knowledge of the life of the bees. With the same design he invokes the sugar which was coming, during the sixteenth and early seventeenth centuries, to replace honey as sweetening for the fruits and vegetables of the Europeans, especially in the northern countries. He compares the harsh experiences of life, when met devoutly, to the sour and bitter fruits which turn in the mouth to velvet when mingled with sugar. Religion is designed to lead us towards tender ways. It can deprive even tragedy of its sting, and keep those who feel they are suffering injustice moving in the channels of love and hope.

Delight, even a measure of sensuous pleasure in delight, is made the inspiration of God, and not, as with so many of the Calvinists, the temptation of the Devil. François de Sales looked with indulgence on a certain coquetry. When the veil that the women of the Visitandines should wear was under discussion, he not only attended the final fittings, he took the scissors in his own hand to help make the garment appear as modish as possible.[1] A sentence by one of François de Sales' biographers brings out the distinction between the saintliness of the scholastic age and the new more temporal saintliness which this concern with fashion reveals: 'On n'imagine pas semblable souci chez Saint Bernard.' Redemption for François de Sales comes partly in resisting, when sinful, overt commitments to pleasures; but it comes still more from the positive infusion of charity, supported by tangible beauty and even a measure of luxury, into all that we do and think. 'No other saint ever built supernatural perfection as much on natural perfection and balance.'[2]

[1] Leclercq, *op. cit.* p. 34.
[2] *Ibid.* p. 36.

Infusion of charity into modern reality

The *Traicté de l'amour de Dieu* has never been called a profane book. Unlike the *Introduction à la vie dévote*, it is not concerned with the experiences of daily life. François de Sales' object is to create in the human soul the most perfect feeling of love for God. L'Abbé Brémond emphasized in his long literary history of religious feeling, that this book is an expression of mysticism in its purest form. But the union with God is achieved by very different means from those of Saint Theresa or Saint John of the Cross.

Dans la plupart des entreprises à la conquête mystique de notre pays, pendant la première moitié du XVIIe siècle...se découvre l'inspiration d'une femme. Ce phenomène constant, cette loi presque absolue n'a rien qui doive surprendre ni gêner un esprit sérieux, encore moins, un esprit chrétien.[1]

The reader is continually led by analogies with the passion of love as we know it here on earth, to the love of God. Thus François de Sales seems to be saying, that those feelings that draw men and women together, when purified, are the most perfect examples of charity that we can know for certain as part of tangible experience. They exist not to be fought off, not to be denied, but to be gloried in when that is legitimate, to be sublimated where that is necessary, to be accepted always in the spiritual sense, as shafts of light which God vouchsafes to reveal the perfection of the eternal love that has been promised us. They can be authentic only when it is the soul that is primarily engaged, when the soul guides the body. They are the supreme examples of love of the neighbour. And this love of the neighbour becomes with François de Sales almost the invitation to the love of God for Himself which is man's first and last opportunity.

This treatise, like almost all of François de Salès' work, is related to his meetings and spiritual friendships with a few women of the nobility, first and foremost to his association with the lady who was Madame de Sévigné's grandmother

---

[1] Henri Brémond, *Histoire littéraire du sentiment religieux en France depuis la fin des guerres de religion jusqu'à nos jours* (Paris, 1916), II (*L'invasion mystique, 1590–1620*), 36–7.

and whom we know as Sainte Jeanne de Chantal. The first time he saw her he is said to have recognized in her the person God had revealed to him in a vision.[1] François de Sales has left it as part of the record, in one of the letters he sent her, that 'le livre de *L'Amour de Dieu* est faite particulièrement pour vous'.[2]

It was they together who founded, in 1610, the order of the Visitation at Annecy. In conception it was novel in many ways, and it was designed to comfort the infirm, to penetrate to all who suffered in the temporal world. As the Père Ignace Armand wrote to François de Sales, 'L'on dit que vous dresserez un hôpital plutôt qu'une assemblée dévote'. The nuns were not to enter a convent, but to visit the poor and give them spiritual and bodily help. While the founders were obliged, under pressure from the Church, to abandon their original plan and to live in convents, the idea contained in this foundation of a lay order of nuns, giving bodily and spiritual help and guidance to those who suffer, was carried out a few years later by Vincent de Paul and the women who helped him.

As a child of poor peasants, Vincent de Paul inherited none of those direct connexions with the nobility which were a part of François de Sales' inheritance. But he had no difficulty in reaching the same kinds of persons and sharing his mission with them on the same intimate terms. That mission was inspired in the same way, by Christian charity. Only with Vincent de Paul the material sides of charity occupied the central place. The power of the new methods and the new ideals to transcend the social barriers, which were real enough in the economic sphere to preclude the entry of a member of the ancient French nobility into trade or manufacturing, is demonstrated by the career of 'Monsieur Vincent' himself, as everyone came to call him.

Some of the original ideas of the Visitandines and the Filles de la Charité were derived from the Ursulines and the

---

[1] Monseigneur Julien, *St François de Sales* (Paris, 1929), p. 117.
[2] Brémond, *op. cit.* II, 583.

Jesuits, orders founded early in the sixteenth century, in the atmosphere of the Reformation, within the Roman Church. But in conception, the Visitandines, and in practice, the Filles de la Charité, went far beyond those preceding orders in bringing the Christian virtues, Charity above all, into the life of lay communities.

The Filles de la Charité carried out fully one of the ideas which had been in the mind of François de Sales and of Jeanne de Chantal in founding the order of the Visitation. A lay order of women, like the Visitandines, the Filles de la Charité, dedicated themselves to the service of the sick, the miserable and the old. But not necessarily for life, like the older monastic orders. They were expected to engage themselves only for a year at a time. They wore no veils or special uniforms. Monsieur Vincent was always reminding them: 'Mes filles, votre charité est un voile qui constitue une protection plus sûre qu'une armure.' Nearly all the safeguards which had ordinarily surrounded the religious were eliminated. And the fact that they were thus eliminated in connexion with a woman's order is especially significant. Safeguards had been regarded as indispensable above all for women, subject as they so readily were to assaults on their virtue. Nothing perhaps could be more symbolic of the reduction of the barriers between the city of God and the city of man, of the entry of Christian ideals into the daily experience of the laity.

The remarkably rapid growth of this new order, combined with the influence of François de Sales' teaching, in France, throughout Europe and overseas, gave a new meaning to the Christian faith in terms of the realities of the world in which we live. These movements of the faith had a deep influence on the history of France and of Europe during and after the middle decades of the seventeenth century. Partly inspired by the issues raised by the Reformation and by the Protestant insistence on the religious significance of temporal life, independent of the sacraments, the work of François de Sales and

Vincent de Paul did much to humanize the harsh and austere sides of Protestantism, as dominated by the followers of Luther and Calvin. The Quakers and the Unitarians are examples of sects, founded in the seventeenth century, which owed much to the gentleness, the tenderness, the compassion, the charity and love to which the French priests managed to give such positive content.

Nowhere perhaps was the influence of this renewal of Christ more dramatic than on the fields of battle and in those distant parts of the world which the Europeans were colonizing. It was a matter of special satisfaction to Vincent de Paul that the Filles de la Charité took over responsibility for tending the wounded in war, a function hitherto left without much success to camp followers. They went even to distant Poland.

Ah, mes filles [Monsieur Vincent exclaimed], y-a-t-il rien de pareil à cela! Avez-vous jamais ouï dire qu'il se soit fait chose pareil? Pour moi, je n'ai jamais vu cela, et ne sache pas qu'il se soit trouvé aucune compagnie qui ait fait les œuvres que Dieu fait par la vôtre.

The great missionary movements of the seventeenth century were mainly independent of these two French priests. But the spirit in which the missionaries worked, at their best, was the same spirit that François de Sales and Vincent de Paul served so single-mindedly. The notion of spreading the gospel by peaceful penetration to all human beings everywhere was novel. We find an expression of it in a small book printed in the mid-seventeenth century proposing as a practical programme that all Jews can be persuaded to become Christians, and to form a 'corps d'Église', as part of a movement to convert all men on earth to the Christian faith.[1] What made such a programme appear both desirable and possible was the new temporal content which the great spiritual leaders of the early seventeenth century were giving to Christianity. That was at the root of the efforts of missions sent out to the ends of the earth.

[1] Isaac La Peyrère (?), *Du Rappel des Juifs*, n.p. 1643 (Newberry Library, Chicago, 4. 616. 484), pp. ii, iii, 153–4.

Infusion of charity into modern reality

Into the Near East, into distant China and Japan, and into newly discovered North America, the Jesuits went, to be followed by Protestant missionaries. They faced the danger of the Indians and the distant Orientals with a willingness if necessary to die for Christ, never to kill for Him. This inspiration was in extraordinary contrast to the European Crusaders of the twelfth and thirteenth centuries, with their brutal atrocities. For a short period of time the Jesuits managed to convince a fair number of Orientals that the civilization which was forming in Europe represented a higher level of human endeavour than had as yet appeared on this planet. The impression, alas, was frequently short-lived, as guns and uninspired businessmen too often belied the promise of the early emissaries of Christ. But it has never been entirely effaced. Upon its renewal and amplification the future of civilization in the atomic age may to a large degree depend.

We are now in a better position to understand what spiritual inspiration was doing for those crude and violent habits which prevailed among the Europeans in the times of Rabelais and Montaigne, and which took the form of such ugly cruelty and violence in war, and especially in the civil wars which accompanied and embittered the religious divisions of Europe. It was largely through women, first of all a few saintly women, that the priests carried their new piety into the temporal world. The appeal of Saint Theresa and of Saint Ignatius was to men much more than to women; the appeal of Saint François de Sales and Saint Vincent de Paul was much more to women than to men.[1] Behind every important step taken by those two priests we find one or more distinguished women, who give and receive inspiration from the new movement dedicated to the redemption of the Christian life here on earth.[2] This dependence on woman for the union of the

[1] Leclercq, *op. cit.* pp. 55–6, 100; Theodore Maynard, *Apostle of Charity* (London, 1940), pp. 130–1.
[2] Julien, *op. cit.* pp. 149–50, 164, 191, 211; Maynard, *op. cit.* pp. 132, 135–6, 141, 151; Emmanuel de Broglie, *St Vincent de Paul*, 3rd ed. (Paris, 1897), pp. 51–2.

spiritual and the material was accompanied by a new sense of the dignity of woman. Potentially half the human race were given larger and more immediate opportunities for redemption than had existed before. They were emancipated from a part of the subordination to men which had always been their lot, or rather perhaps we should say they were offered a new glory, that of inspiration and leadership through the special virtues of their nature, in their spiritual relations with men. These virtues were those of the will and the sensibility more than of the intelligence.[1] At a time when the scientific revolution was beginning to orient the intelligence away from the specifically human problems which had concerned the great Greek and Scholastic philosophers, the inner human experiences were permeated by those judgements of intuitive love and conviction of which women in their finest moments have provided the great examples. As a result a tenderness and a moderation were infused into temporal life hitherto lacking.

The discovery of woman was among the principal achievements of the heart and the imagination, as well as of the Christian faith, during the very period when the scientific mind was moving in new directions hitherto never extensively explored. One wonders whether the development of these new riches in the *human* species was of any less importance for the coming of industrial civilization than the discovery of new truths in the physical and biological sciences.

The emancipation of woman, which was so remarkable a part of seventeenth-century European history, has been largely ignored in recent times. This is perhaps partly because the new curiosity of man during the last hundred years for his own past has been accompanied by a different kind of movement towards the emancipation of woman, the feminist movement. That movement aims to give women equality with men, to enable them to do all the things that men have done and do.

[1] Cp. Leclercq, *op. cit.* p. 55.

Infusion of charity into modern reality

The late Artur Schnabel, one of the great musicians of our time, was fond of telling stories about remarks made to him in his dressing-room after concerts. One of his favourites concerned an irate woman he had never seen before who rushed at him one night, without preamble, and demanded in a loud voice: 'Why *are* there no great *women* composers?'— almost as if he were personally responsible. Schnabel thought for a moment and then answered quietly and reassuringly: 'They have better things to do.' The emancipation of women in the early seventeenth century was in that spirit. It was at the heart of the new search for Christ. It may be said to have aimed to give women, not equality, but superiority in those spheres of life in which they are the masters: in the capacity to give, in the capacity to suffer for those they love. This emancipation was above all a work of love, a work in which love itself was given a new dignity and a new spiritual dimension in the temporal world.

Just after the middle of the seventeenth century, a Parisian named Antoine Furetière wrote a book, *Le Roman bourgeois*, in which one of the characters describes this innovation. Mischievous Cupid, as a kind of spirit, escaped from the heavens where he feared the wrath of his mother, Venus, and of his grandmother, Thetis. He found an asylum on earth among a company of friendly shepherds and shepherdesses. Perhaps out of gratitude for their kindness to him, perhaps out of pity for their ignorance, he left his mischief behind. He conferred on mortals, through the intermediary of these shepherds and shepherdesses, the art of making love.

For, if you are not aware of it [runs the story], until this time love was unknown among men; all the unions had been made heretofore after the fashion of animals, for the purpose only of reproduction. This beautiful passion of love, insinuated in human hearts, which gives such great joy, and which serves to unite souls more than bodies, was still ignored on earth.[1]

---

[1] Antoine Furetière, *Le Roman bourgeois* (Paris, 1868), p. 138.

We are led to infer that this meaning of love was for human beings an invention. Stendhal was to call it a *miracle*. 'L'amour est le miracle de la civilisation', he wrote in the early nineteenth century. 'On ne trouve qu'un amour physique et des plus grossiers chez les peuples sauvages ou trop barbares.'[1] With the materialistic meanings within which the word 'invention' has come to be confined in recent times, Stendhal's choice of a word is perhaps more appropriate, for it is necessary to call the attention of a modern audience to the fact that miracles do occur in history beyond the domain of natural science and technology. Furetière does not tell us when this miracle occurred. But as we look back, we can see that it was a part of the revolution in the standards for the conduct of temporal life that was taking place at the juncture of the sixteenth and seventeenth centuries.

We have had occasion to dwell in this chapter on the religious origins of this revolution. By carrying the devout life outside the cloister and potentially into the experience of every human being capable of embracing it, by assigning the primary role in this movement to women, love was infused into the experiences of daily life to a degree unequalled before this time.

The Middle Ages had given Europe supreme examples of Christian devotion beyond the world. The Renaissance had given Europe supreme examples of the delight in the world that the search for beauty and charm can provide. A great spiritual achievement of a few innovators in the early seventeenth century revealed the possibility of joining the two. Their union—the union of the highest ethical ideals with the delights of secular art—was necessary for the attainment of the higher level of politeness and cultivation of which Gibbon was to write in the eighteenth century, for a partial attainment of the virtues which Mirabeau considered essential elements of 'civilization'.

[1] *De l'Amour* (1822), ch. xxvi.

V

THE AESTHETIC BASIS OF CIVILIZATION

Any close acquaintance with the lives of artists or with the history of the arts will suggest that the pursuit of beauty has by no means always been accompanied by the pursuit of virtue. It is little wonder, therefore, that in many minds a moral life and a life devoted to art almost exclude each other.[1] I was conversing recently with an American woman, who has tried her hand at writing poetry, and who has had some acquaintance with professional writers from the times of the First World War, while retaining an active life as wife and mother. I asked her what characterized an artist. I discovered he was for her a person unreliable in keeping engagements, who drank to the point of becoming an alcoholic, who practised irregularities in matters of sex—in short a thoroughly untrustworthy creature.

I. THE RENAISSANCE CULT OF DELIGHT

I was reminded of that conversation when I came recently on Lord Macaulay's views concerning the Italian world in the times of Machiavelli, the late fifteenth and early sixteenth centuries. In that age the search for beauty had become almost the principle of existence; Vasari contended that it might be possible again to equal but never to surpass in aesthetic perfection the architecture, sculpture, painting of those times. For the persons to whom Machiavelli addressed his writings, almost all problems, even those of government and of war,

[1] The problem has been touched on recently by Jacques Maritain in his *Creative Intuition*. He discussed it directly in some lectures that he gave in the autumn of 1952 for the Committee on Social Thought at the University of Chicago. The substance of these lectures remains to be published.

were approached as if the solution were to be found in art. The important matter was to achieve a neat, elegant, brilliant result either in the mind, on paper, or in the visual arts.

In his essay on Machiavelli, Macaulay wrote as the early Victorian that he was.

Habits of dissimulation and falsehood, no doubt, mark a man of our age and country as utterly worthless and abandoned. But it by no means follows that a similar judgement would be just in the case of an Italian of the Middle Ages. On the contrary, we frequently find those faults, which we are accustomed to consider as certain indications of a mind altogether depraved, in company with great and good qualities, with generosity, with benevolence, with disinterestedness. . . . The character of an Italian statesman seems, at first sight, a collection of contradictions. . . . We see a man whose thoughts and words have no connexion with each other, who never hesitates at an oath when he wants to seduce, who never wants a pretext when he is inclined to betray. . . yet his aspect and language exhibit nothing but philosophic moderation.[1]

Macaulay's essay provides an excellent introduction to Machiavelli's play, *Mandragola*.[2] As a piece for the theatre the work is beautifully constructed with remarkable economy of words and speed of action. It reads almost as freshly today as it must have read 450 years ago.

What are its ethical implications? It elicits the sympathy of an audience with the seduction of a beautiful young woman, inclined to virtue, by the most unscrupulous deceits, in which the priest who is her confessor aids the lover who betrays his friend, the woman's husband. Of course the moral effect of a work of art on the beholder is unpredictable: so much depends on the basic character and the temporary condition of the individual affected. It is possible for a work whose ethical *intentions* are above reproach, even the Bible, to be used as a justification for evil by a weak man; it is possible for a work whose ethical intentions are vicious, for example a piece of pornographic writing, to fortify the virtue of a strong man.

[1] Thomas Babington Macaulay, *Critical and Historical Essays*, 1 (London, 1843), 83–4.   [2] Machiavelli, *Mandragola*, ed. Stark Young (New York, 1927).

The Renaissance cult of delight

This play of Machiavelli's, like most of the art which developed in Europe during the fifteenth and early sixteenth centuries, mainly under Italian inspiration, lies well between the extremes set by revelation and the pursuit of the obscene. Its object is to incite human beings towards neither God nor the Devil; it is to delight an audience by the story and by the manner in which that is presented. But it would not perhaps be going too far to suggest that, in so far as standards are involved, *Mandragola* is lacking in the finer shades of ethics. At any rate this has frequently been suggested, not only about Machiavelli, but about all the Italian literature of this brilliant period in art.

There is as great a contrast between these conditions concerning the ethical implications of art and those which came to prevail in the Victorian Age, in Lord Macaulay's time, as there is in the conscience of the Europeans concerning 'atrocities' in the early sixteenth and the late nineteenth centuries. How was the change brought about? What part had it in the 'civilization' in which many Europeans came to take such great pride? What part had it in providing the 'stable general culture' which the last Victorian economist, Professor Pigou, regarded as a prerequisite for the economic order of free enterprise that prevailed in Europe and North America during the Victorian Age? In short, had the artistic history of the late sixteenth and early seventeenth centuries, like the religious history, an important part in laying the cultural foundations for industrialism?

2. TOWARDS AN ETHICAL CONTENT

The tradition of sacred art as it came down from twelfth- and thirteenth-century Europe, and as we still see it in the subjects then treated by artist-craftsmen in cathedrals, churches and monasteries, was to distinguish sharply between good and evil, and to represent, often in terrifying terms, the consequences of sin.[1] But, as with the overwhelmingly urgent

[1] Cp. Elinor Castle Nef, *Letters and Notes Volume I* (Los Angeles, 1953), pp. 46–7.

desire for saintliness among some men and women in the Middle Ages, the battle between good and evil was fought almost entirely in relation to the problem of salvation in the world to comé. Art in the main was then not secular but religious, and by virtue of that fact, it was a part of the city of God on earth, not unlike the monastic life. And, along with the declining integrity of monastic life, the distinction between good and evil in sacred art was weakened during the fourteenth and fifteenth centuries.

The Reformation was carried through partly because of a renewal of the vitality of Christian ethics. Among the Protestant leaders and their more ardent followers, this was combined with a sense of responsibility to overcome the ethical indifference often characteristic of even the priest and the monk in the later Middle Ages. The Reformation was also carried through with a determination to lay greater stress than ever before upon good moral conduct in the temporal world. With the early Protestants, especially with the followers of Calvin, and particularly with the Puritans in England and the Presbyterians in Scotland, the renewal of a strong ethical conscience was combined with objections to many forms of religious art as idolatrous,[1] and with objections to many forms of secular art as immoral. Calvin said mass first of all in the open air, laying his Bible on a rock, without any ornament. Protestant influence on the whole, during the hundred years which followed the Reformation, did less to purge art of vicious implications than to shrink the sphere of art in the life of Europeans and to disparage those spontaneous desires for pleasure and delight which are mainly good.

The stress of religious guidance during the middle and later decades of the sixteenth century was on the fall of man, on the depravity of human nature, as the result of original sin. Such an outlook encouraged a rather extreme reaction against the freedom of inspiration on which the greatest art of Europe had thrived during the hundred years preceding the

[1] See above, pp. 46–7.

Reformation, and down through the great works of Rabelais, which were first published in the fifteen-thirties. Ethical neutrality had been characteristic of an age in which men, especially in Italy, made a cult of beauty, to which no doubt actual sensuous experience contributed strongly. The Renaissance culminated in a sweep of syphilis and Protestantism over Europe, and both were evidence of depravity to the increasingly dogmatic Roman Catholics. There was a disposition, in consequence, to treat the impulses which had nourished art, along with the loosening of monastic life, as responsible for both syphilis and Protestantism. Delight in beauty and in all the joys to which earthly life introduces us through our senses, came to be regarded as vicious in itself. Somewhat as Saint Theresa reacted violently against the slackening of the discipline of the cloister, the Counter-Reformation in some ways attempted to outdo the Protestants in ethical discipline.[1] And here the effect promised to be more far-reaching, because ecclesiastical foundations largely retained under the Roman Catholic communion their immense wealth and their patronage over artistic works of every kind.

These elements in the Reformation persisted into modern times. But in the very period from about 1580 to 1660, when religious feeling was infused into the temporal order through the inventions of leaders like François de Sales and Vincent de Paul, equally remarkable and complementary inventions in secular art tended to a degree that was novel to make delight the ally of virtue, of compassion, and so of moderation and tenderness in manners. This was one of the great achievements of European letters, of European painting and music. At a time when ethics and art seemed on the point of being divorced from the spiritual life of the Europeans, the three realms of human experience were brought together in a new way by the fresh content given to literature and painting, by

[1] Cp. Charles Dejob, *De l'influence du Concile de Trente sur la littérature et les beaux-arts chez les peuples catholiques* (Paris, 1884), pp. 268 ff.

the fresh emphasis laid on perfection of form, on elegance, order, moderation and clarity in all the visual arts from architecture to sculpture, as well as in music, poetry and prose.

What were the innovations? First of all the contribution of letters was in no way inferior to that of religious sentiment in the new dimensions which it gave to the qualities of woman and to the love that some women inspire. In his novel, *Le Roman bourgeois*, Furetière suggested, it will be remembered, that a fresh spiritual meaning was infused into human love by the descent of Cupid among friendly but uncouth shepherds and shepherdesses. Furetière gives us no idea when this occurred, but it is evident that he was thinking of pastoral literature, which goes back to the Greeks. In the second half of the sixteenth century there was a renewal of it in Europe. The French pastoral novels (of which *L'Astrée* of the marquis d'Urfé is the most celebrated, as it was by all odds the most read[1]) were not the first to appear, but it is probable that Furetière wrote with them mainly in mind. Urfé is supposed to have taken a great deal from the two most successful examples of Spanish and Italian pastoral literature, the *Diana* of Montemayor and the *Aminta* of Tasso. That he was influenced by these works, as were other French writers of pastoral romances, is certain. But that they gave him the exalted ideal of love expressed in some passages of *L'Astrée* is hardly possible, for it is not to be found, so far as I can discover, in either of those works. The book 'is profoundly French and it was inspired pre-eminently by French aspirations as they were forming around the year 1605'.[2]

Aminta is superior to any French pastoral novel as a work of art. So probably are the best English poems which employ pastoral subject-matter—Spenser's *Shepherds' Calendar* and Sydney's *Arcadia*. But the precious side of pastoral literature, with the new dignity it assigned to love, was a French innovation. It is common to call Urfé's works and other

---

[1] M. Magendie, *La Politesse mondaine et les théories de l'honnêteté en France, au XVIIe siècle, de 1600 à 1660* (Paris, n.d.), p. 168.　　[2] *Ibid.* p. 176.

romances in the same vein by contemporaries of his, *romans précieux* rather than *romans pastorales*.

Urfé was almost exactly a century Machiavelli's junior. His book is indicative of a great change that was taking place about a hundred years after Machiavelli in the relations between art and morality. Except for Montaigne's *Essais* and François de Sales' *Introduction à la vie dévote*, *L'Astrée* was perhaps the most influential book in France during the early seventeenth century. Even after the advent of the great French classical literature, it is always cropping up in correspondence, in the correspondence of Madame de Sévigné for example.

The book is immensely long, and today it makes weary reading. It is in five huge parts. The first three came out while Urfé was alive, beginning in 1610; the last two after his death, finished by his secretary Baro, who was later one of the original members of the French Academy. As eighteen years elapsed between the publication of the first and the final part, many persons read the book in instalments, as they were to read Proust almost exactly three hundred years later.

It is not unnatural to draw comparisons between these two long literary works and between the influence they may have had on their contemporaries. Some of us of the generation which is now passing through middle life know of the tremendous impression that *A la Recherche du temps perdu* made upon our ways of looking at the people about us, the towns they lived in, the resorts they frequented, the morals they practised, the art some of them sought to achieve. We became more closely aware of characters like Swann, the duchesse de Guermantes, Saint Loup, Charlus, Madame de Verdurin, Bergotte, than of many persons we actually knew. We talked of them to each other as if we had seen them every week on terms of intimacy. Life in the little town of Combray assumed a reality for us which affected our own childhood memories. The hotel at Balbec became more real to us than any hotel in which we had actually stayed. We saw Elster's paintings of the lower Seine valley more vividly than Monet's. *La petite phrase* of Vinteuil echoed in our ears more frequently than familiar notes of Debussy.

So may it well have been with *L'Astrée* three hundred years earlier. That was a time when conditions of living changed far more slowly than from 1910 to 1960; it was a time when there were relatively few distractions to compete with reading for those who read. As Geoffrey Scott has taught us, the written and the printed word then possessed a prestige which they now lack.[1] So the public for *L'Astrée* extended to almost everyone among the small number of persons who read. This meant that it extended to most of the persons who influenced social and political and religious, as well as artistic life: to the nobility, the clergy, the civil servants who formed the *noblesse de robe*, and some of the merchants.

From 1610 to 1660, readers of *L'Astrée* lived in their minds the lives of the shepherds and shepherdesses, Céladon, Astrée, Silvandre, Hylas, for example, as they appear in this description of 'honnête amitié'. Many of these readers felt more at home out-of-doors in the rolling country, with its natural delights, that Urfé created for them than in their own châteaux, town houses or workshops. Some actually outfitted themselves in pastoral garb and took to the fields in their native provinces.

What were the ideas of the *romans précieux*? In what directions did they draw the new taste that was forming, and the ethical standards that were being combined with taste? Much as François de Sales and Vincent de Paul built their religious orders around a fresh concept of the role that it was open to woman to play as a spiritual force in temporal life, the novels of which *L'Astrée* provides an example derived their influence from a fresh ideal of womanly perfection and of masculine honour. This complemented the ideal that was forming at the same time with the spread of the devout life.

Silvandre, the shepherd, speaks in the third part of *L'Astrée* of women as having so great a superiority over men in their

---

[1] See *The Architecture of Humanism*.

powers of inspiration that they are the natural intermediaries between human beings and the heaven that, it is hoped, awaits them. Women, Silvandre says, 'give birth to the finest thoughts of men'; who can doubt 'that God has placed them on earth to draw us toward...eternal happiness?'[1] The love evoked by this concept of woman arouses human beings to an immense spiritual effort *not* to submit to those animal instincts which the common run confuse with love, but to conquer the instincts in the interest of the highest norms of human hope. As Astrée says, it is by doing voluntarily what is painful and contrary to our undisciplined impulses, 'that we show ourselves to be reasonable and not sensual'.[2] The devotion of man for woman can have its incomparable spiritual fulfilment only when physical desire is restrained and controlled in two ways. First, by fidelity to one woman. 'He who can imagine that it might be possible at times no longer to love, is already no lover.'[3] Secondly by the primacy of spiritual love.

Silvandre asks Hylas, 'Why would you have it that love, which illuminates our understanding and forms the thought of our soul, should not give the body those desires which are natural to it?' He then draws a distinction which brings out the capital point of Cupid's instruction, as that was to be described later in Furetière's novel. 'The body,' says Silvandre, in speaking to that grosser character, Hylas, 'is not excluded from love; those who love as I do, feel the desires of which you speak, because they are in love; those who love as you do remain on the level with the animal, they love only because they have those desires.'

So the gift of the body becomes a symbol and an expression of the prior gift of the soul. Through the soul, the total love that the human being instinctively feels for the self is ennobled by being felt for another, even by being transferred to that other. Total giving is inherent in woman's

---

[1] *L'Astrée*, III (Paris, 1624), 878.
[2] *Ibid.* IV, 770.
[3] *Ibid.* I, 216.

8-2

nature more than in man's, and in this respect she is man's spiritual superior. In Héloïse we have the great Christian example of the loss of all sense of self, or perhaps it is more exact to say of the total merging of the self in Abélard. But the extreme heroism Héloïse exhibited and which led her to the cloister, became in the new concept of early seventeenth-century literature a possible staple of life as led here on earth. It is open to any two persons who feel deeply enough and who make sacrifices enough for the sake of each other, and above all for the sake of the spiritual mission which unites them, to live an almost sacred life in the temporal world. '...Tout en respectant le caractère souverain de l'amour de Dieu,' wrote one of the most sensitive historians who has studied the early seventeenth century, 'ne peut-on pas dire qu'en transportant ce sentiment des hauteurs du ciel sur la terre, les précieux n'ont pas changer la définition qu'on en pourrait donner? On aime la femme comme on aime Dieu.'[1]

The example provided by those few rare unions in which these exalted hopes were fulfilled with a large measure of success, played a part in history. It was a novel part, because for the first time the search for spiritual perfection and the desire for delight could be fused without any concessions to immorality in action or even in thought and imagination, as they were fused towards the end of the seventeenth century, according to Saint-Simon, in such marriages as those of the duc and duchesse de Chevreuse and the duc and duchesse de Beauvillier. It was an effective part, because such rare unions lift and immensely magnify the effects of individual virtue in the two participants. Supreme testimonials as they are to the power of the human being to give, their influence on those who witness and on all those who hear of them and share in them is to strengthen charity, compassion, moderation and the deeper justice which is tempered by those virtues.

When this concept of a partial fulfilment of the highest spiritual hopes was beginning to establish an important

[1] Strowski, *St François de Sales*, p. 409.

place in literature, the much older concept of knightly
chivalry had all but disappeared. Cervantes was writing
its epitaph in his great book at the very time when Urf
began his much longer, and by comparison tiresome stof.
There is a sense of unreality—in terms of the reality fat
gradually assumed the centre of the stage after the thirtenth
century—about medieval romances. Chivalrous forts of
conduct were not carried effectively into daily life, as the
politeness and restraint of seventeenth-century french
literature was at least partially carried into the day life of
the European nobility, to be spread thence, though requently
no doubt in a diluted form, to persons of dignity irevery class
of society. The chivalrous romances often reflet the age in
which they were written, with heads swept from their bodies
to float through the air. In so far as the ideds of medieval
chivalry were concerned, they seem to have btained little or
no substance in the temporal life of Europe. Don Quixote
was a fanciful character, no doubt, but the picture Cervantes
gives us of him is something more than a lampoon; these ideals
existed only in the person of exalted and partly crazy men.

The ideals of classical French literature were much more
sensible. The new chivalry was soon established on a much
firmer basis than the old.

During the generation that immediately followed Urfé and
François de Sales, the union of high ethical standards with
the search for beauty became an essential part of aesthetic
inspiration. Thus virtue and art were joined in a fresh way
after it had seemed that the worship of art for its own sake in
the spirit of the Italian fifteenth century, and the eschewing of
art as corrupt in its essence in the austere spirit of Luther and
especially of Calvin, might put an end to that union between
the sacred and the beautiful which was the glory of European
experience from the eleventh to the fourteenth century.
The new union of the sacred and the beautiful, achieved in
Europe in the seventeenth century, was a more secular, a
more earthly union. It did something to repair the wounds

inflicted on the soul as well as the body, by the separation of
he religious life from the common life in the world, for the
ʰul was now coming (because of the changing nature of
relity) to be more affected by the body, at the same time
tha through the new saintliness, it was acquiring a new
conﬁence in its immediate relation to Christ. The exquisite
and te restrained became a part of the content of art, as we
observ most perfectly perhaps in the novels of Madame de
Lafayetᵉ. In the tendencies and implications of their plots,
her storiᵉ associate the most exquisite womanly beauty with
the defenᶜ of her virtue. Take, for example, the way in which
she brings ut the moral of her short novel, *La Princesse de
Montpensier.* Finding that the news of her affair with the
duc de Guise vas being spread about everywhere was a death
blow for the pincess. 'She could not bear the pain of having
lost the esteem ᵈ her husband, the heart of her lover and the
most perfect of frends. She died in a few days in the fullness
of life. She was ᵒne of the most beautiful princesses in the
world, and she migḫ have been the happiest, if all her actions
had been guided by virtue and prudence.'

In a different way, and with the supreme art of the poet,
the new moderation and restraint are expressed in the dramas
of Corneille and Racine The ancient plots of classical Greece
and Rome are so modiﬁed and softened that the more gruesome aspects do not appᵉar; the slaughter takes place whenever possible off the stage

This restraint is expressed in the wit of Molière, a wit
which is always at the service of rational control and moderation
of our instincts towards passion and violence. This we find
in the lines of *The Misanthrope*, where the hater of human
vice is cautioned against excess:

> La parfaite raison fuit toute extrémité
> Et veut que l'on soit sage avec sobriété.

In the content of literature as it developed especially in
France during the seventeenth century, we have a kind of

summons to the *honnête homme* to rise out of himself, and, while finding an outlet in the world for his emotions and even his idiosyncrasies, with calm and self-control to be better than he is. This summons complements that contained in *The Introduction to the Devout Life*.

The efforts to achieve greater secular realizations of reason, of tenderness and moderation, of charity and compassion, of justice, were not confined to France or to literature. It was perhaps in painting that artists introduced a new humanity with the most touching results. The greatest painters of the period from about 1600 to 1660, especially those in whose works the content of painting is of the greatest importance, were not French. They were Flemish, Spanish and Dutch: Rubens, Velasquez and Rembrandt. In them we find expressed the new aspirations of European spiritual and cultural life towards charity and compassion, and towards a more tender treatment by human beings of each other. Both aspirations were essential to the partial realization in temporal life of Christian ideals.

Rubens' life, from 1577 to 1640, stretched right across the years when the spiritual and aesthetic basis was being laid for the civilization which facilitated the triumph of industrialism. No artist of those times had more direct experience in the diplomatic counsels of Europe than he. Close to the deeply religious Infanta Isabella, the daughter of Philip II, who governed the Spanish Low Countries, and who almost forced him on her nephew, Philip IV, as a negotiator for peace with England, Rubens painted a great ceiling in the Louvre for the French queen-mother, Maria de Medici. The choice of an artist for this task was Richelieu's. But, as my colleague Otto von Simson has suggested, 'it seems as if the artist did win the last round against the statesman. . . .The catholic universalism of Rubens' vision'[1] perhaps made a deeper mark on history—by its contribution toward 'civilization'—than the artful strategy (necessarily corrupted by complete dependence on material realities) of the greatest contemporary European

[1] 'Richelieu and Rubens', *The Review of Politics*, VI, no. 4 (1944), 451.

statesman. Rubens' political activities were not a pastime from his painting, nor was his painting a pastime from his political activities. He was no Churchill; but he revealed a quality that it is more difficult for even a Churchill to achieve in our time or perhaps for one who is primarily a statesman to achieve at any time: the capacity to integrate a many-sided life with compelling effectiveness in a spiritual direction.

In 1637–8 Rubens painted a picture called 'The Horrors of War', now in the Pitti Gallery in Florence.[1] He had been commissioned to paint it by a powerful Italian family, probably the Medici, and when it was finished he had it boxed and shipped to Florence, then a journey of some weeks. It occurred to him 'that a fresh painting, after remaining so long packed in a case, might suffer a little in the colours'. Consequently he wrote to the Flemish painter, Justus Susermans, who had settled in Florence, asking him to put matters right, 'and if need be...[to] retouch it wherever damage or my carelessness may render it necessary'. Any notion we may have that the meaning of the picture was a matter of indifference to him as an artist is dispelled by Rubens' letter which was written for the purpose of facilitating Sustermans' task.

The principal figure is Mars, who has left the open temple of Janus (which in time of peace, according to Roman custom, remained closed) and rushes forth with shield and blood-stained sword, threatening the people with great disaster. He pays little heed to Venus, his mistress, who, accompanied by her Amors and Cupids, strives with caresses and embraces to hold him. From the other side, Mars is dragged forward by the Fury Alekto, with a torch in her hand....On the ground, turning her back, lies a woman with a broken lute, representing Harmony, which is incompatible with the discord of War. There is also a mother with her child in her arms, indicating that fecundity, procreation, and charity are thwarted by War, which corrupts and destroys everything. In addition, one sees an architect thrown on his back with his instruments in his hand,

---

[1] He apparently left more than one version, since there is another in the National Gallery in London.

to show that that which in time of peace is constructed for the use and ornamentation of the City, is hurled to the ground by the force of arms and falls to ruin.... That grief-stricken woman, clothed in black, with torn veil, robbed of all her jewels and other ornaments, is the unfortunate Europe who, for so many years now, has suffered plunder, outrage, and misery, which are so injurious to everyone that it is unnecessary to go into detail. Europe's attribute is the globe, borne by a small angel or genius, and surmounted by the cross, to symbolize the Christian world.[1]

War is always a horror, in the language of the nineteenth century an 'atrocity'. There are plenty of war pictures before the seventeenth century, which depict the 'horrors' of war on the field of battle. But they are descriptive. It was for purely descriptive ends that Leonardo da Vinci, in his note-books, gives directions for drawing or painting a battle. Rubens' picture has a moral purpose. It is an allegory designed to awaken Europe to the folly of the total wars that were being waged. It draws attention to the damage done by war to all those virtues which human beings at their best strive to serve in temporal life.

The new and more ethical view of the dangers of total war as an offence to the charity after which sensitive Europeans were beginning to strive, appears at about the same time in a different form in the painting of 'The Surrender of Breda', by that other very great *European* painter of the early seventeenth century, Diego Velasquez. This picture was finished some eight years after the event had occurred in 1625. It is designed to emphasize the responsibility of men to restrain their violent impulses even in the heat of battle and of victory. The charitable response of the victor, the marquis of Spinola, is chosen as the central theme. We are moved by the tender, the almost compassionate manner, in which he returns the sword of the defeated Dutch governor of the fortress.

Breda marks the beginning of a new movement towards

---

[1] *The Letters of Peter Paul Rubens*, ed. Ruth Saunders Magurn (Cambridge, Mass., 1955), pp. 408–9.

limited warfare, in which fighting is more and more restricted by a sense of the obligation to fight battles according to polite rules, and to treat the enemy as comrade and almost as friend, once the battle is over.[1] This movement is an example of the transfusion of the sense of charity and love into the life of the temporal world through the medium of painting.

Nowhere in the history of painting are these supreme human aspirations towards the reparation, through the spirit, of the tragedy to which we are all condemned by our mortality, brought out so touchingly or so permanently as in the works of Rembrandt. When I spoke just now of Rubens and Velasquez as the two great *European* painters of the seventeenth century, I had not forgotten Rembrandt. But Rembrandt is essentially the painter of *humanity*. One may even speak of him (and he has in fact been spoken of) as *the painter*.

A friend of mine told me of an experience that he had recently in the Rembrandt room of the Metropolitan Museum in New York. He was looking at a characteristically moving canvas, a bust of Hendriskje Stoffels. He became aware of a couple standing a little behind him who were looking at the same picture. As he looked the word 'compassion' welled up inside him. At that moment, just when the word flashed in his mind, he heard the woman murmur to her companion, 'What a sense of compassion in the mother!' No other word seemed so fitting, and to the work of no other painter can that word be applied with the same force as to some of the supreme works of Rembrandt, for example his 'Christ at Emmaus' or his 'Good Samaritan'.

The works of the very greatest artists are in a real sense beyond time. That is what binds art to the eternal. But they are created by men who are also in time, otherwise they would be disembodied. And the greatest works of Rembrandt, though unique and timeless, were conceived in time, as part of the great seventeenth-century movement to bring into the world the deepest charity, inspired by the Founder.

[1] See my *War and Human Progress*, especially ch. VI.

Towards an ethical content

The arts of literature and of painting were acquiring a Christian content that was novel in connexion with actual temporal life at the very time when the proportion of the subjects derived from Scripture was diminishing. Charity and compassion were descending to earth at much the same time as love. Upon the union of these, and the union of them all with justice, upon the growth of the integrity of the given word in matters of public and of international law, the coming of 'civilization' in no small measure depended.

3. TOWARDS GREATER CLARITY

The coming of civilization depended also upon the spread of good form in the arts and in the art of living, upon a clarification and a discipline in the instruments used by artists in achieving their results in every media. On the eve of the religious wars, the future of literature, especially in France, was bound up with the invention and the eventual diffusion of subtle rules of correct usage, of style and of eloquence. The age that followed, which was the age of such extraordinary innovations in the methods of scientific inquiry, and which was also the age of Shakespeare and Donne in England, of Malherbe and Guez de Balzac in France, was an age during which the use of language and the ways of writing changed with astounding speed, at least among the French, the Dutch and the English.

A Frenchman of the twentieth century finds it difficult to understand even with the aid of a dictionary the prose of Rabelais, who died in 1553. The prose of Montaigne, who died in 1592, presents certain odd turns of words and phrases which the modern discipline of French grammar and syntax does not prepare us to follow. But the words, the cadence, the phrases in the prose of Pascal, who died in 1662, and who was less than a hundred years younger than Montaigne, seem almost as natural today to a Frenchman of the older generation as the prose of Anatole France, and possibly a little more familiar at first acquaintance than that of Proust. Montaigne has, I understand, been translated into modern French, but, so far as I am aware, no one has thought it necessary to perform such a 'service' for Pascal.

A parallel alteration seems to have taken place in connexion with Dutch literature. In the history of Holland the period from about 1580 to 1660 was not only the greatest period in Dutch painting, but the greatest period in Dutch letters. The poetry and prose of such masters as Vondel speak to the Dutch today almost as directly as the poetry and prose of Malherbe and Corneille, of Pascal and Bossuet speak today to the French.

The change in the character of English prose during these decades was perhaps less surprising than the changes in the character of French and Dutch prose. But there is a gulf between the style of Latimer and Hooker and that of Milton and Dryden. All of us feel at home with Shakespeare, with Francis Bacon and the King James version of the Bible, and still more with the language of the Restoration, as we never feel at home with the English of Chaucer or even that of the Reformation.

Our European ancestors moved a long way between about 1580 and 1660 from what is to us unintelligibility to intelligibility in their use of language. And much the same thing happened in some countries in the ways of writing and spelling out words.

Partly because of the scarcity of material on which to write during the Middle Ages it had been necessary to develop a script which would enable men to pack as much as possible into a small space. At least from the seventh and eighth centuries in Europe, the need for economy in the animal skins, then much used for writing, had led to the use of narrow letters instead of broad, to a small script and to as many abbreviations as possible. During the Middle Ages writing had been mainly an art for the few—practised frequently with great distinction and sometimes with genius.[1] It was a kind of elegant shorthand.

---

[1] Compare the valuable discussion of handwriting by E. A. Lowe in *The Legacy of the Middle Ages*, ed. C. G. Crump and E. F. Jacob (Oxford, 1926), pp. 205–19.

Towards greater clarity

That was still the condition during the sixteenth century. The historical researcher today who wants to read documents written in the age of Henry VIII or of Elizabeth I must undergo special instruction in palaeography or at least teach himself by painful and careful disciplined concentration usually over a period of weeks. The signs for letters, the ways of indicating double letters, the spelling, the signs for numbers and the ways of using numbers, the manner of forming the letters, all are alien to him. This is not a question of legibility or of the clarity of the script. Even the most elegantly formed letters, even the most beautiful and perfectly preserved pages before and during much of the Elizabethan age, are inaccessible for reading purposes to the untrained modern eye.

Yet by the reign of Charles I, English manuscripts are by comparison clarity itself, if the individual who composed the document had an easily legible hand. How frequently our correspondents today apologize for sending us typewritten letters, by remarking that we could not decipher their words if they resorted to longhand! The art of handwriting is now preserved only by the very few—mostly by a very few cultivated women of leisure. So, many of the multitudinous written records that have come down to us from the mid-seventeenth century are more intelligible to our eyes than the scrawls of our contemporaries. I came recently on a report concerning some researches of a friend of mine made more than thirty years ago. His wife, who had had no training at all in reading old documents, accompanied him on a research expedition to archives in the north of England.

The Dean of Durham [she noted], to whom Frank had long before written for permission to examine his manuscript collection, received us with the most unexpected good fellowship. We worked with the MSS. in the morning and I by good luck found a most valuable tax account book [of 1636] full of information that we wanted, with interesting figures. I have scarcely since recovered from my elation or my astonishment in discovering that *I was able to read it.*[1]

[1] Elinor Castle Nef MSS. Category I, Letters, August 7, 1924, in Archives of the University of Chicago.

Can this remarkable change in the intelligibility of manuscripts early in the seventeenth century be explained in terms
of physical facilities for getting larger numbers of letters on
a page? Was it simply that paper had become available in
sufficient quantities to make any kind of shorthand unnecessary?
If this were the principal explanation, we should expect the
change to have begun sooner.

The period in Europe from about 1470 to 1550 was one of
very rapid increase in the output of paper, which had at least
to keep pace with the need which arose from the multiplication
of printing presses in Germany, Switzerland, France, Italy
and the Low Countries. As paper became cheaper and much
more plentiful on the Continent, as the scribblers also increased in number, corruptly written manuscripts seem to
have increased rapidly too. Many notaries' books in France
in the sixteenth century are practically unintelligible to the
trained palaeographer, not because of the character of the
script but because of the carelessness and slovenliness of the
handwriting. So one may say that the growth in the output of
paper encouraged bad, hasty handwriting. But the movement
towards the presentation of letters in a way that is intelligible
to us today began later, at a time, from about 1600 to 1640,
when the growth in the output of writing paper in Europe
was much less impressive than it had been a hundred years
earlier.[1]

The pressure for economy in the letters put on a page seems
to have been lifted, therefore, some time before the spelling
out of words in full. Nor was the movement towards modern
script at the beginning of the seventeenth century universal
in Europe. In Germany the older Gothic script, inherited
from the Middle Ages, persisted until recently. And in
Germany there was in the early seventeenth century no such
sharp change towards modern intelligibility in writing or in

---

[1] While the output of paper grew much more rapidly from 1580 to 1640 in England
than in continental countries, most of the paper produced was of rough quality, suited
only for such purposes as wrapping. Up to the time of the Civil War most of the paper
used in English books was imported.

style as took place in France, Holland and England. This suggests that the principal explanation of the turn to what seems to us intelligible handwriting is to be found in the changes in the ways of thinking and in the use of language which were taking place during the same decades in those countries which were foremost in the politics of Europe, and also in economic innovation and development.

In France above all the movement towards clarity and elegance, in writing and in speech, was part of a general movement to bring order and style into all the arts, as part of a further movement to bring order and style into the art of living. During this very period François de Sales and Vincent de Paul were rescuing the devout life from the civil strife and the indifference to religious feeling characteristic of the second half of the sixteenth century. They were giving the search for moral perfection a meaning in connexion with temporal life that it had never had before. This was the time when principles and rules of orderly composition were being invented in painting and architecture, in the making of furniture and tapestries and in the composition of music, as well as of poetry and prose. A whole series of tongues of delight was created in an age when the order and restraint, the moderation and the variety, which the new styles made it easier for the artist to practise, were essential to the new ethical content of works of art.

Continental experience, under the leadership especially of France, was moving in the early seventeenth century in the direction of a new perfection of form and subject in all the arts, better suited to good ends than the pursuit of delight as that had been carried on during the late fifteenth and early sixteenth centuries, under the leadership especially of Italy.

How were these developments in the arts related to the industrial history of Europe? What part did they have, along with the innovations in spiritual life, in the coming of 'civilization'? What had the coming of 'civilization' to do with the triumph of industrialism?

CIVILIZATION
AND INDUSTRIALISM

I. A NEW ECONOMY OF DELIGHT

The origins of what has been called 'classicism' in European art, the coming of the Baroque styles, need to be understood as an integral part of an industrial development characteristic of most continental states, a development differentiated from that characteristic of Great Britain and Sweden during the period from about 1580 to 1640. The earlier movement of industrial growth, animated primarily by the search for beauty, which occurred at the time of the Renaissance, above all under Italian example, was playing itself out in the old age of Titian and Michelangelo, at the time when the French religious wars began. It had penetrated deeply into the economic experience of almost every country from Spain to Bavaria and Saxony. The end of the sixteenth century and the early decades of the seventeenth were marked in Spain as well as in central Europe, and to a lesser extent in the Spanish Low Countries (modern Belgium), in Franche-Comté (not yet part of France) and in Italy itself, by a collapse of the prosperity that had revolved around the Renaissance cult of delight.

That was the very period during which, as Ranke suggested a century ago in his *History of the Popes*, the European aristocracy, at least on the Continent, acquired a new position of dignity, grew in wealth, and within the structure of the rising national states in political, social and religious influence. If the late fifteenth and much of the sixteenth century can perhaps be described as 'the age of the despots', the late sixteenth and the first half of the seventeenth century should be thought of not only as the age of royal absolutism but of the rise of the nobility. Hand in hand with the growing authority of the aristocracy went the new disposition to give an ethical content to art, and to work out formal rules for the achievement of beauty in all the arts.

As a consequence the stimulus to industrial development provided by the new search for artistic perfection differed from that provided by the old. In order to build, to furnish and to decorate the palaces, the châteaux and the town houses of the nobility, the civil servants and the merchants, it was necessary to fashion new furniture, new hangings and ornaments of many kinds. Fine houses grew in number especially in the towns. Apart from the palaces of great sovereign princes, among whom the king of France was the greatest, they diminished in size. The new houses were more easily susceptible, when they changed hands, to renovation and renewal, than the vast private houses of the Renaissance, such as the palace of Jacques Cœur at Bourges. The new rooms were more intimate; their decorations were more exquisite. These rooms were the setting for beautiful objects, such as the musical instruments, which were no less works of art than armour had been. These were mainly played in the quiet of private homes; there was no way of giving them a place, even an ornamental one, on the field of battle!

Much of Europe turned in the direction of a renewal and an extension of an economy which sought to supply, first and foremost, the requirements of delight. In France and Flanders, partly under Italian inspiration, and to a large extent also in Holland, it was the industries which aimed at beauty and provided the ornaments for elegant and polite living which came into their own between the fifteen-eighties and the sixteen-forties. The primary objectives of the industrial economy of the early seventeenth century were to give a new form and perfection to buildings, to furniture, to musical instruments, to clothing and bedding, to carriages and boats, and to decorations of every kind, to make these objects, by means of aesthetic inventions, more commodious, more comfortable, more perfect for the purpose for which they were intended, and to increase the number of such commodities in as far as this was consistent with the maintenance and the improvement of their quality. A new *élan* was given to qualitative progress, which was destined to continue into the eighteenth century.

France became (along with Holland) the leading country of Europe for the luxury and the artistic industries. That was partly a result of considered policy. The French crown favoured these industries as over against the heavy industries of coal-mining and iron metallurgy. For example, an ordinance of 1543 extended the tax on iron to all forges in the realm, and also declared that, in the interest of conserving the forests, the *number* of iron mills should not be increased.[1]

There was only one group of metal commodities in which French demand grew from 1540 to 1640 more rapidly than English. These were fine artistic wares—such as ornamental balustrades, window grills, entrance locks and knockers, and locks and decorations for strong boxes—such as were suited to the new style of living which the French were initiating, and which were, as a consequence of the new alliance of art with the ethical and the spiritual, part of the effort to bring the devout life, Christian charity and love into the temporal world. All these objects of artistic craftsmanship contributed to a new sense of style; they enabled the persons who were forming taste in polite society to have commodities in almost perfect taste, and this facilitated their purpose.

The cutlers who forged the knives and razors for courtiers and for other wealthy people, mounted them in exotic wood, tortoise-shell, mother-of-pearl and ivory. They mastered the craft of manipulating all these materials, as well as iron and steel. In doing so, they were confronted with the need for invention which engages the artist as an individual whenever he is at work, for each work presents its own aesthetic

---

[1] Archives Nationales, X^{IA} 8614, ff. 22–3. For details concerning this policy, see my *Industry and Government in France and England* (Philadelphia, 1940), pp. 83–8.

problems. The fashioning of metal ornaments required much skill and patience, a fine sense of aesthetic values, elaborate and varied labour. But the amount of metal consumed in the process was small. Three tons of pig iron a year were regarded as an adequate supply for the shop of a steelmaker in Dauphiné in 1660,[1] and such shops sometimes produced swords and the metal faces for sickles and scythes as well as the fine steel for artistic cutlery. Racine (and Diderot after him) said that the achievement of the artist consists in creating a world out of nothing. That is why the results of artistic industries do not show up in the statistical estimates of which modern economic historians, fired by the disposition to calculate all values in quantitative terms, have come to make something of a fetish.

It was for the sake of such artistic results that a great portion of all the industry of continental Europe came to be carried on in the early seventeenth century. The move in Great Britain, in Sweden, and to some extent in the shipping and shipbuilding industries of Holland, towards industrial production mainly, if not exclusively, for the sake of a flood of cheaper wares, was the exception, not the rule. The industrial revolution of early modern times was an experience limited largely to the north of Europe and especially to Great Britain. At the end of it, on the eve of the Civil War, England, Scotland, Sweden and Holland had altogether perhaps ten million inhabitants, hardly as many as greater London today, out of a total population in western Europe of some sixty or seventy millions.

The effects on workmanship and consumption of the new goals of labour-saving and the multiplication of output were limited even in those northern countries. The Dutch developed the artistic industries simultaneously with industries like shipbuilding. There was a demand for elegant wares in Great Britain which was satisfied mainly by imports, but which contributed to the formation of English taste. Even before

[1] J. B. Giraud, 'Les Épées de Rives', *Documents pour l'histoire de l'armement au Moyen Âge et à la Renaissance*, II (Lyons, 1904), 245.

the Civil War a manufacture of fine wares with imported silk began.

Europe was left, then, at the end of the so-called religious wars, at the time of the peace of Westphalia, in 1648, with at least two developing industrial economies. The inclination of our contemporaries, with their scale of quantitative values, is to see one of them alone as progressive, as leading towards the industrialism of the nineteenth and twentieth centuries. The inclination of our contemporaries is to regard the other as holding back progress.

Years ago, when I was beginning my researches among documents pertaining to industrial development in England and France, I had the valuable help of an assistant brought up in the United States. Although she had been trained as a scholar concentrating in classics, Greek in particular, she held, in company with almost all scholars of her generation, the current ideas concerning technical progress. She measured it, not in terms of contributions to beauty, to goodness, to spiritual perfection, but in terms of contributions to efficiency and material productivity, matters which are determined quantitatively. We were then engaged, she and I, in studying documents pertaining to industrial organization and technology in England and in France under the *Ancien Régime*. She was not unnaturally impressed by the difference between the industrial evolution of the two countries. She remarked that in its development France was almost invariably two or three generations behind England.

Is this true? If we are concerned only with those realizations in industrial life which were leading *directly* towards power-driven labour-saving machinery and mass production, it is at least partly true. A good case can be made for the contention that France was left more and more behind England in the late sixteenth and early seventeenth centuries. Industrialism, as the world has now come to know it, required a concentration of effort upon labour-saving machinery and the exploitation of natural resources such as coal and iron, and later oil and hydroelectric power and rubber, to provide the heat and the raw materials necessary to turn out an avalanche of commodities. There is, therefore, one sense in which the search for quality, which was still central to the economic development of most of Europe in the seventeenth century, the priority given to delight as the goal of manufactures, imposed a brake on progress towards industrialism. It takes time to make beautiful things. In the life of the artist there are no short cuts. The rhythm is dictated by the nature of the work; inventive ingenuity is directed not to making commodities cheaper in larger quantities but to obtaining more perfect results. A fundamental difference exists, therefore, between the kinds of inspiration, the kinds of thought, manual effort and organization required in the two cases.

But the question is whether both were not needed in order to bring into being the modern world of quantitative values, vast populations and massive output. The contributions of labour-saving inventions, large capital accumulations, and administrative skill in organizing ever larger ventures in industry, commerce, transportation, communications and finance, are obvious. These alone have been considered by historians. Many of them have come to the conclusion, not altogether correctly as we have seen, that the early seventeenth century was a time of sluggish progress in industry and especially in industrial technology. If we consider Europe as a whole at that time, it is certainly true that inventions in the realm of faith, in the realm of art and of artistic craftsmanship were more impressive than mechanical inventions.

The predominant economy of Europe in the mid-seventeenth century was not the budding quantitative economy which had made notable progress in the north and especially in Great Britain. It was the economy of quality, in which continental nations excelled. During the hundred years that followed—at least until the seventeen-thirties and forties—the new-found interest in quantitative growth and in the technical improvements necessary to nourish it was never lost. The scientific revolution became an ever more important part of European intellectual life. Modern scientific methods, and the scientists who employed them with striking results, acquired an enormous prestige at a time when the works of the mind were more respected and more influential than perhaps at any other period in history. In the early eighteenth century no *king* was held in greater esteem and even awe by intelligent Europeans than Newton.

Nevertheless the making of fine wares retained the centre of the stage. In spite of the increasing importance which many men on the Continent attached to the new sciences, the time had not yet come when the increasing desire in all continental countries to imitate the labour-saving techniques which the English had cultivated with special emphasis during the half century preceding the Civil War, took precedence over the disposition to seek perfection in the fashioning of a relatively small number of commodities. Throughout the seventeenth century and at the beginning of the eighteenth, science (especially the order, discipline, clarity and elegance of the French mathematicians) was placed at the service of artistic perfection no less than at the service of astronomy and physics, and even more than at the service of labour-saving technology.[1]

Both the Scots and the English were inclined to be conscious of the fact that their continental neighbours—and especially the Italians and the French—regarded them as uncouth and barbarous. Benvenuto Cellini had compared them to wild beasts. This attitude of condescension was a little like that which the Anglo-Saxons later, during the nineteenth and twentieth centuries, in the security of their phenomenal quantitative progress, were to adopt towards the Latins. In the seventeenth and early eighteenth centuries the English were fascinated by the fine wares that came from abroad. After the Restoration they may almost be said to have become more

[1] See for example René Taton, *L'Œuvre Mathématique de G. Desargues* (Paris, 1951), pp. 60–3.

interested in improving the quality of native manufactured goods than they were in constructing steam engines, in extending the use of coal in smelting ores, and in the development of transport by rail. Does this not help us to understand why there was so long a lag between the times when the English first addressed themselves to these problems (1590–1610) and the successful practical solution of the most urgent among them (1780–1800)? In the interval, and especially from the sixteen-forties to the seventeen-forties, the English, the Scots and the Irish were prone to follow *continental* example when it came to industrial inspiration, almost if not quite as much as the French and Germans came to follow *English* example after about 1700 in the mining, the metallurgical, the glass-making and eventually the textile industry, as they came also to follow English example in matters of agricultural technique. The admiration of the inhabitants of the British Isles for the charms of fine living, and for the industrial organization that goes with them, was at least as strong in Newton's time, when living had in fact become more charming, as when Edward Smyth introduced the 'precious French wares' of Jean de Lespine towards the end of Elizabeth's reign. After the Civil War the English made remarkable progress in the production of goods of quality. They excelled the continentals in some of these, such as flint glass and playing cards. These improvements in industry in Great Britain went hand in hand with a development of the visual arts—the art of painting, the art of landscape gardening.

The disposition of economic historians to regard the preoccupation of the Europeans with an economy of quality as a stumbling block in the way of the eventual triumph of industrialism is one-sided. There is an important sense in which the dedication of the Europeans to the construction of a beautiful Europe, by the strengthening of fine craftsmanship in the service of the crown and the various ranks of the nobility and higher bourgeoisie, was essential to industrialism. The economy of quality was an integral part of those cultural foundations of industrial civilization that we have been seeking to discover and to describe.

This was not an economy imposed on Europe and America by French political hegemony.

One must be either a liar or a fool [wrote Bernanos] to suggest that the modest armies of Louis XIV subjected Europe to French classicism as a form of slavery. Civilized humanity chose classicism and the culture and spiritual hope which went with it, because civilized human beings found themselves at home in it. Having classicism enabled them to breathe more freely, to understand and to live with each other better.[1]

Civilization, in the sense in which the word was invented, provided an essential framework for the spread of industrialism, and in that sense civilization hardly existed in the mid-sixteenth century. If it had come to exist to some extent in the mid-eighteenth century, that was partly because of the prior place given by the Europeans to the *new* economy of quality. This was born at the juncture of the sixteenth and seventeenth centuries. It helped to civilize the Europeans and to prepare them for industrialism, in at least two ways.

The dedication of so many Europeans to the making with the hands of beautiful things as the central principle of economic endeavour prepared Europe and America for the eventual triumph of power-driven machinery and mass production. That triumph was based on the progress of the human soul towards greater dignity and integrity, expressed tangibly in the novel store placed on the value of human life, on the commodities which serve the peaceful and cultivated needs of men and women, and on a reduction in violence. The progress of the human soul was not a function of the modern technological progress, which became sensational in the nineteenth and twentieth centuries; rather it helped to create

[1] Georges Bernanos, 'Redevenir humain', *La Nouvelle Relève* (Montreal, September 1941), pp. 10–11. (I have made a rather free translation of these sentences.)

conditions that encouraged such progress. In so far as man's search for liberty and integrity expressed itself in the making of beautiful things, this provided a novel incentive to the eventual production of commodities in much greater quantities than ever before. At the same time the fashioning of exquisite objects helped to liberate human energy eventually for peaceful mass production because it contributed in a variety of ways to the concept and the practice of limited warfare.

In order to arouse the intense interest in the multiplication of durable commodities and conveniences, which has characterized the nineteenth and twentieth centuries, it was necessary not simply to demonstrate the possibility of increasing the output of cheap goods, with the help of mineral fuel, cast and pig iron and sheet glass; it was necessary to show that a much larger number of exquisite commodities could be made, that an expansion of a qualitative economy was possible. The furniture, the household conveniences and the ornaments of the few with means had to be of a kind that the many, with their hopes of comfort and delight, would want to possess. Some of the many had even to savour directly the charm offered by these ornaments. Citizens of modest position were already beginning to do so, at any rate in Holland, by 1640. In that year we have an account of the Dutch townsmen by Peter Mundy, who travelled extensively both in Europe and Asia. Of these citizens he wrote:

All in general are striving to adorne their houses, especially the outer or street roome, with costly peeces, Butchers and bakers not much inferiour in their shoppes, which are Fairely sett Forth, yea many tymes black-smithes, Coblers etts., will have some picture or other by their Forge and in their stalle. Such is the generall Notion, enclination and delight that these Countrie Native[s] have to Paintings Allsoe their other Furniture and Ornaments off their dwellings very Costly and Curious, Full of pleasure and home contentment, as Ritche Cupboards, Cabinetts, etts., Imagery, porcelaine, Costly Fine cages with birds etts., all these commonly in any house off indifferent quallity; wonderfull Nett and cleane, as well in their houses and Furniture, service, etts., within doores, as in their streetes.[1]

It is evident that even in modest homes, already before the middle of the seventeenth century in parts of Europe, models were being provided by artists and artist-craftsmen, which the mass producer later on, with the help of machinery and large-scale business organization, could imitate and multiply. The beautiful objects which Mundy describes, provided an incentive for the later expansion of production.

During the seventeenth and eighteenth centuries, with the help of the new artistic craftsmanship, a style of living spread through Europe that led all Europeans to want to share, at least to some extent, in that *douceur de vivre*, accompanied by high *standards* of virtue in actual living, which a very considerable few were coming to possess for the first time in history. So the growth of an economy of quality made the idea of increasing production much more attractive than it would have been if all Europe had turned to making cheap commodities with the help of coal and cast and pig iron at the end of the sixteenth century, when the cheap commodities were as crude and rough as the prevailing manners, and when almost no attempt had been made to perfect them with the help of art.

In order to understand the contribution of the economy of quality to more stable and humane relations between individuals and nations it is necessary to remember that, in the midst of the religious wars, some Europeans were beginning to believe, as a result partly of the attempts to infuse spiritual perfection into temporal life, in the feasibility of achieving religious objectives more effectively by persuasion than by force. Partially successful efforts to demonstrate the effectiveness of persuasion beginning at the end of the sixteenth century helped to orient the European mind towards limited

[1] *The Travels of Peter Mundy in Europe and Asia, 1608–1667*, R. C. Temple ed., IV (1639–47) (London, 1925), 70–1.

warfare, at just the time when the developing economy of quality blunted the cannon and other firearms, by concentrating attention on their appearance rather than on their killing properties, and provided the furniture, the musical instruments and the decorations suited to a polite style of living. An example of the new efforts at peaceful solutions of vital religious issues is afforded by the struggle between Protestants and Catholics to win over the district of Chablais in the last decade of the sixteenth century. An example of the new efforts to perfect social relations with the help of art and artisanry is afforded by the rise of the *salon* in the decades that followed.

2. THE 'PEACEFUL CONVERSION' OF CHABLAIS

At the end of the sixteenth century, parts of the lands bordering Lake Geneva had been in dispute for nearly two generations, politically as between the Swiss and the dukes of Savoy, and in the matter of faith as between Protestants and Catholics. One of the principal struggles had been over the country known as Chablais, which stretches from the outskirts of Geneva to Evian, and includes the hills and mountains which rise above the shores of Lake Geneva.

After the Swiss conquest of 1536 the Chablais had gone to the Protestant Bernois, and the local population had been won slowly but, as it seemed, thoroughly for Protestantism, by the victors. They forbade the practice of the Catholic faith on pain of fines, exile and the confiscation of property. When the Chablais was given back to Savoy in 1564, by the treaty of Nyon, the price which the Bernois had exacted was the retention of the Protestant worship by the inhabitants, and the exclusion of the Catholic. This put the dukes of Savoy in a difficult position. A Catholic sovereign was obliged, by treaty, to resign himself to the persistence of heresy within a part of his dominions. At a time when politics was inextricably mixed with religion, it was almost an accepted principle of

139

government that to be a good subject a person must practise the religion adopted by the prince.

In 1580 a new duke, Charles-Emmanuel, inherited Savoy. Dedicated zealously to Catholicism, he sought for a way of getting around the treaty of Nyon. In 1589 he took up arms to defend his political position against an invasion of Chablais by a coalition of French, Genevese and Bernese forces. In the treaty that followed their defeat, the reformed religion retained its ascendancy, but the number of Protestant temples was restricted. Once this treaty was signed, the Roman Catholic bishop of Geneva sent in a flock of fifty priests to convert the population. They were backed up by the arquebuses and bombs of the duke. But by this time, after a half century of practice, the reformed worship had become deeply in-grained among the people, and as soon as the troops and their firearms were withdrawn, the converts returned, in the words of the Catholics, 'to their old slime' (*à leur bourbier*). They were encouraged, it seems, by the entry into Chablais of Genevese and French troops, whose appearance put all the remaining Catholic priests to flight.[1]

Up to this point the pattern was the habitual one of the Wars of Religion. Faith was on the side of the strongest battalions.

For those who felt that a religious minority constituted a threat either to the power of the sovereign or to the salvation of the people, or to both, was there, as the French 'Catholics' had been claiming in their controversy with the 'English' Catholics, an alternative to 'strangling heresy'? Could a Protestant stronghold be won over to the Roman Church without the use of force? The question was of great interest in all states, especially in states governed by Catholic princes with considerable Protestant minorities, and above all in France where negotiations were beginning between the rival religious groups, destined to lead to the limited toleration of Protestants provided a few years later under the Edict of Nantes.

At the beginning of the year 1594 François de Sales, after

---

[1] Strowski, *St François de Sales*, pp. 80-2.

a long preparation as a student in Paris and in Italy, had taken up his first post as a priest of the chapter of Geneva. Here he was on the very threshold of the lands of Chablais, which he had known as a child and young man. He decided to see what he could do to settle matters there peaceably in favour of the Roman faith. In September 1594 he went unarmed and alone, except for his brother Louis, into the Chablais, bent on settling down in the capital town of Thonon, where the Calvinist was the only worship permitted by the local government. The bishop of Geneva was hard up; he could not finance an expeditionary force; but it cost him nothing to encourage the mission of this young priest.

The first months of François de Sales' mission resulted in few if any conversions. He expressed his dissatisfaction with the results he was obtaining at Thonon in a letter written on 7 April 1595:

> Voici déjà le septième mois, et toutefois ayant prêché en cette ville ordinairement toutes les fêtes, et bien souvent encore parmi les semaines, je n'ai jamais été ouï des huguenots que de trois ou quatre, qui ne sont venus au sermon que quatre ou cinq fois....[1]

He was approaching the point of despair. His original hope that he would have only to hold mass and that the local people would recognize how superior it was to Calvinist services, seemed to be an illusion. He changed his tactics, and began to make a personal appeal to individuals. He used the connexions of his Savoyard family to meet some of the local Protestants, to converse with persons whose history, character and preoccupations he knew something about. He talked to them quietly and reasonably, treating them not as lost souls threatened with perdition, but as seekers after truth like himself, who were either misguided or intimidated by Calvinist threats of violence. In this way he was able to enter into direct relations with the most intelligent, influential and powerful men in Chablais.

---

[1] *Ibid.* p. 84.

His first conquest was of a lawyer, Poncet, famous for his learning throughout the region. Poncet had been pursuing the study of theology on his own account, and he had already begun to doubt his Calvinism before François de Sales came to Thonon. The main stumbling blocks to his conversion were his fear of the Bernese Protestants and his uncertainty in the matter of philology, especially as it related to the Gospel.

The great missionary, like the great artist, is able to convince some people of the truth of ideas they already half hold, but have been impeded by propaganda or restraints from adopting. Thus he liberates them to become what they have partly wanted to be all along, and so they move in the new direction not only without regrets but with joy. François de Sales was learning this lesson about the human heart, and it was a lesson that he was to put to immense use. He worked with skill and sympathy to reassure Poncet, to lead him to forget the worldly fear of violence that the Calvinists had kindled in him. So eventually he was confirmed in beliefs to which his learning already had drawn him. On 20 April 1595, hardly two weeks after François de Sales had written his discouraging letter concerning the lack of response to his sermons, Poncet renounced the Calvinist worship.

His conversion was followed shortly afterwards by the partial conversion of the leading personage of the Chablais, Antoine de Saint-Michel, the baron d'Avully, whose influence in local government was immense, one may perhaps say decisive. By the end of summer Avully, without formally becoming a Roman Catholic, had broken down the opposition among the local syndics to listening to François de Sales' sermons.[1] Henceforth the young priest was at least assured of a hearing.

In his efforts at persuasion he did not confine himself to the spoken word. He prepared and distributed leaflets written in longhand. Years after his death these papers, which he began in the winter of 1594–5, were published under the title

[1] *Ibid.* pp. 88–90.

Controverses. They had been conceived as part of a book, and they were written with greater attention to elegance of phrasing than either of his two famous works which were so widely read. The *Controverses* demonstrate the new, disciplined French style, which was being forged already at the end of the sixteenth century.[1] In striving to make himself clear, François de Sales achieved, at a cost of much labour and pains, remarkable simplicity, elegance and charm. He addressed himself to the entire local population of Thonon, in the hope that those who could read would transmit the content of his argument to the others. He wrote, as he spoke, with a moderation and a good sense that would blunt such wounds as his desire to convert might inflict. He appealed directly to the Bible, above all to the New Testament, the very source upon which the early reformers had been accustomed to rest *their* case.

For two years, until the autumn of 1596, the duke of Savoy had abstained from any use of force. Then he intervened with the arms which had become so familiar and so fearful in religious controversy. His soldiers entered Chablais. Those among the local population who refused to change their faith were punished by exile and by the confiscation of their wealth. Chablais became Roman Catholic.

There has been much debate ever since as to whether or not the conversion of this country was brought about by force. The considered words of the most judicious modern student of the episode seem to be close to the truth: 'The pacific methods and the subtle and skilful persuasions of the early period were rendered much more efficacious when they were reinforced by others, including exile and the confiscation of wealth.'[2]

François de Sales' opposition to the use of forceful methods by the duke is only a pious legend. Yet there is a sense in which he never abandoned his mission of peaceful conversion. He had no direct part in the use of force. It was not he but other priests who participated in the new methods of conversion

---

[1] *Ibid.* pp. 99–104.   [2] *Ibid.* p. 108.

under duress. In his personal actions he continued the pacific ways he had introduced during the first two years of his residence, and thus reaffirmed the value of substituting persuasion for force.

The Chablais experiment was turned to account in establishing a kind of mystique of voluntary conversion. The legend grew and spread that the little country had been won back entirely by the new, virtuous and pacific means on behalf of which the French 'Catholics' had already appealed in their writings. The good tidings were carried rapidly all over France by word of mouth and by pamphlet. One pamphlet written at Thonon in 1598 and printed at Lyons in 1599, bears the title 'Agreeable News for all good Catholics of the voluntary conversion of the greater part of the Duchy of Chablais and other parts adjacent to Geneva, to our holy faith and religion, Catholic, Apostolic and Roman'.[1] The news made an impression throughout Europe.

It is rightly a preoccupation of the scientific historian to push his inquiry into the facts as far as it will go, and to distinguish what actually happened from what is falsely said to have happened. But do the facts of history that can be established tentatively, by means of tangible verifiable documentation, give us the truth of history considered as a whole? Do they not sometimes leave out what is most essential in the processes by which human beings have evolved as individuals and as members of society? Here a deeper probing into the facts is often quite inadequate to settle controversial matters. It may, when pursued without imagination, actually confuse the historical issues which are at stake. 'Il y a deux sens parfaits', Pascal wrote, 'le littéral et le mystique.' Would it be enough to state with respect to the episode in the history of toleration which François de Sales' mission in the Chablais represents, what is in terms of scientific history true, that the title of the pamphlet published at Lyons gives a false picture of what actually happened? To leave it at that, if we are

---

[1] Newberry Library, Chicago, D. 4038. 018.

seekers after historical truth, would be to ignore two things no less important than a precise recital of the facts. First, legends about an event, when they are believed, may have even more influence on history than the facts. The legend of voluntary conversion in the case of Chablais strengthened the hope that religious ends could be achieved by persuasion instead of force. Secondly, scientific historians are inclined to be the children of their time, and their time has not been that of the Wars of Religion. In the nineteenth century, when scientific history came into its own, the practice of converting people to one branch or another of Christian worship by force of arms had become almost unthinkable. Consequently scientific historians, in considering the times of Philip II and Henry IV, are likely not to recognize how great an innovation was involved in such efforts at peaceful persuasion in matters of religion, or how important for the establishment of 'civilization' was their *partial* success.

3. THE 'SALON'

In the decades that followed the conversion of the Chablais, in the teeth of the terrible events of the Thirty Years War, the Europeans were creating a society in which the new ideals of charity, compassion and love, of beauty in the service of those ideals, and of elegance and order, were given material body. Nowhere perhaps were the new efforts at restraint and decency, combined with rational discussion, expressed better than in the founding and the spread of the *salon*. This was a new institution, which provided a most effective means of communicating the ideas contained in the spiritual and aesthetic innovations of the times of Henry IV and Louis XIII, of James I and Charles I. Good manners were gradually beginning to be part of daily life. Polite conduct as a responsibility and a privilege of all honest men and virtuous women began to acquire a *reality* which knight-errantry had never had.

Civilization and Industrialism

In the spring and summer of 1608 an English parson's son from Somerset, named Thomas Coryat, who was a kind of court fool in the reign of James I, travelled all over the Continent, mostly on foot. He recorded his impressions in a book which was published in 1611 under the inelegant title, *Coryat's Crudities hastily gobbled up*. With his gobbling habits, Coryat was surprised to find on his journey into Italy that 'the Italian...strangers doe alwaies at their meales use a little forke when they cut their meat. The reason of this...is because the Italian cannot by any means indure to have his dish touched with fingers, seeing all mens fingers are not alike cleane'.[1] As Coryat moved south, the fork was working its way north. It was from peoples whom the modern Anglo-Saxon is inclined to think especially dirty, from the Italians and the French, that our northern ancestors partly derived the habits of cleanliness and politeness that came into the ascendancy during the eighteenth and nineteenth centuries.

Greater elegance at table was accompanied by greater elegance in the drawing-room, where hostesses now received their guests, and which became the setting for intimate conversation. The *salon* provided a place where thinkers and men of letters met to influence and be influenced by civil servants, diplomats, priests and statesmen. The first famous *salon*, which served as the prototype for so many others, was established in 1615 by Madame de Rambouillet, then a matron of twenty-seven, in the harmonious setting of the newly built Hotel de Rambouillet. She had helped to plan its architecture. Born in Rome, the daughter of the French ambassador, Madame de Rambouillet was one of those who brought the splendour of the Italian Renaissance to France, and helped to cultivate a new splendour and order, with an originality growing out of a fresh concept of universality.

At the time when Madame de Rambouillet was planning and starting these meetings, which were to provide a model for so many others ever since, French society had at its disposal

[1] *Coryat's Crudities*, I, 236.

the new novels, especially *L'Astrée*. In his book, Urfé offered the example of a polished life, based on a high level of intelligence, in which the liberty of a pastoral existence was subjected to strict rules and to the acceptance of precise obligations. The surroundings were beautiful; there was no winter, no snow, no heavy cold; the skies were forever clear, the trees perpetually green, the flowers always in bloom. But *L'Astrée* was a work of fiction. Great ladies, in the presence of the new veneration of woman, conceived the idea of trying to realize its ideals in actual life within the four walls of a beautiful room. The new gentleness which François de Sales and his followers were introducing into Christian teaching, strengthened the purpose of these ladies; they had an increasing number of priests at their side when it came to the development of the *salon*. François de Sales and Monsieur Vincent came and went. Corneille read his plays aloud.

While the modern mind is inclined to look mainly at the snobbish sides of polite society, this association ignores an element which was of decisive importance in its genesis, and which was the very reverse of exclusive. It overlooks the desire of the creators of the *salon* to pay homage to very high standards of virtue. The noble idea expressed by Montaigne, that all men were his compatriots, was parcel of the inspiration that led the great ladies of the seventeenth century to strive towards a perfect spectacle of human relations within their homes, to which the open sesame was nothing less than virtue itself. Madame de Rambouillet is said to have declared that, if a completely good man was to be found in the Indies, a black man, she would spare no effort that would be to his advantage, even if she did not know him.[1]

It is not by size that we can judge universalism. Even the largest drawing-room in the most splendid palace was a small place. But the ideal represented by the *salon* had no boundary of geography or race; nor was there any arbitrary restriction upon the number of *salons*, as there was upon the court; the

[1] Magendie, *La Politesse mondaine*, I, 388–9.

salon could be multiplied as far as there were persons able and willing and wealthy enough to form them. Ideally the only limits were the limits of perfection.

Of course these limits were soon reached. At their best human beings always fall short of virtue, although it does not follow, as the cynicism of the contemporary world would have us suppose, that by serving virtue as an ideal they fail to improve. The very strength of the ideal in seventeenth-century France, made the shortcomings and the vices of many persons who frequented the *salons* especially glaring to the few whose devotion to the good life was authentic.

As the *salons* multiplied, some of these sensitive persons sought asylum from the society they found there. They took not only to the pastures and woods, but to the new religious foundations. In renouncing the world for quiet beside the religious of Port-Royal, Pascal set an example which was followed by some of the purest characters of Louis XIV's reign. He set another example which is almost unique. He gave up the certainties of science for the search for certainty in the realm of faith, for the search for the larger Truth which comprehends every facet of human experience.

In the *salon*, the two realities of our existence were actually combined in a novel way. At its best the *salon* was a work of art. Here was a stage, but a stage on which the actors were persons living their lives. The line between the best theatre and life itself is always thin. French classical drama, as it developed during the seventeenth century, seems unreal only to those who have forsaken the realities of style and form. In actual fact the unity of time and place required by the rules of French classical drama make the transition from spectator to actor seem easy and natural. In the *salon* inner life was almost placed on the level of formal drama. But it was not possible to sit back, as in a theatre, and console oneself with the knowledge that what is going on is only a play. The setting offered an opportunity for an admixture of fiction with experience, of the ideal with the real, which had a pervasive influence both on the arts and on the ways of actual living. It brought the spiritual into the temporal life. And inasmuch as man is a combination of soul and body, the life of the *salon* was in a most important way truer to human nature as a whole than the life that is often supposed to be more real, which is lived without delicacy or restraint.

The whole life of western Europe and America, and of the rest of the world into which Europeans moved, was coloured by this institution. We still practise the manners that were introduced in the early seventeenth century, when we gather at table or in the drawing-room, when we join clubs in Belfast or in Chicago. But we have forgotten the origins of these manners and rules. We have forgotten their importance in spreading the values of honest friendship and of decency in human relations, in contributing to understanding among men and nations, and to the restraints on the animal propensities, the violence, inherent in human nature. Understanding and restraint helped to make the coming of civilization possible.

4. QUALITY AND INDUSTRIAL CIVILIZATION

The efforts to achieve a better temporal world made by saintly men and artists, and by the persons who took those efforts seriously and helped to give them material reality, were interpenetrating during the seventeenth and early eighteenth centuries. The search after excellence in one sphere fortified the search after excellence in all. Manners of the *salon* made their impression upon manners on the battlefield.

In the château at Broglie, in Normandy, where the present duke is one of the world's great physicists, a large picture hangs in the entrance hall. It shows an English general fully equipped and armed, in the act of mounting a fine horse. The inscription tells us that this is a painting by Reynolds of John Manners, marquis of Granby. He was an English commander in the Seven Years War. At that time, the achievements of the Broglie family were mainly military. The then duke was a marshal of France and in 1760 he had taken his principal adversary, the marquis of Granby, prisoner in the battle of Corbach. The painting is a gift which the marquis made the duke after he returned to England, as a token of his esteem and with his grateful thanks for the generous hospitality shown him at Broglie, when he was his host's prisoner!

It is one of hundreds of examples of the new restraints on war, which for a time seemed to have forever banished the concept of total conquest from the earth. One thinks of Goethe's account of his childhood at Frankfurt-on-Main. When the city was occupied by the French, the commanding general lived for a long period in the Goethe household. He became a friend of the child Goethe. Goethe liked him very much and the occupation, which lasted for some time, enabled the boy to perfect his French. It led him to commit to memory long passages from Racine's plays which were in his father's library, and this experience was an important influence in forming one of the three or four greatest European poets, and perhaps the most universal mind that has appeared during the past two centuries on this planet.

The growing restrictions on violence during the seventeenth century were at the roots of the concept of limited war and political stability. They helped to provide a framework of general culture essential to the phenomenally rapid industrialization of Europe and the world during the nineteenth century and at the beginning of the twentieth.

Both the economies which evolved in Europe during the last decades of the sixteenth century and the first half of the seventeenth made contributions to the increasing decency of individual conduct and to the growing moderation in the conduct of international relations. The insistence on quantitative values—accompanied as this was by a movement towards standard weights and measures ever more accurate and precise—was providing a basis for verifying people's reliability in economic relations. The detection and the punishment of the most blatant and obvious forms of dishonesty were rendered easier than in the past by the new precision that was so striking a feature of European history from about 1570 to 1660. The love of truth in the domain open to the natural scientist was helping to create at the same time an inquiring, a sceptical attitude towards men's intuitive assumptions and emotions, which helped to spread gradually an increasing desire for the toleration of other individuals, of other societies, of other races. It provided a safeguard against the excesses of the emotions, which are explosive compounds when they erupt without self-control.

Yet being an honest paymaster and no more is dehumanizing. It is well for us to discipline our emotions. But the disposition to deny them any general validity, which has gone with the triumph of modern science, deprives the human race of instruments that enable men and women to penetrate to the spiritual world, to transcend the limitations of the material things which have come to rule our lives, and to strengthen the character of physical existence here on earth. Developing a critical, a sceptical outlook on life in the end proves sterile. It leads the scholar and the expert to retreat into their increasingly narrow special subjects, and there to indulge in the luxury of continual disagreement with their colleagues.

The verification and cultivation of the highest human attributes—charity, love, honour, justice, clear thinking—depend on the human personality, which the scientist and the statistician leave out of account. It is neither in the rise of modern science nor in the rise of modern economics that the *cultural* foundations of 'civilization' can be mainly found. Their principal sources were the partially successful efforts to practise a Christian life in the temporal world and to bring about an alliance between the quest for beauty and the quest for virtue in a society dedicated to delight. The search for perfection in the art of life was the great achievement of Europe in the seventeenth and early eighteenth centuries. It was facilitated by the search for perfection in the making of commodities, which enlisted all the human faculties in workmanship and inculcated habits of arduous but leisurely composition, so that the tempo of work and the tempo of social intercourse were conducive to creative thought.

The economy of abundance measured by quantities, which began to prevail during the nineteenth century in parts of Europe, the British Empire and America, was not, as has been generally assumed by scholars as well as by the modern public, the basic cause for such spiritual and moral progress as has occurred in modern times. One of the main sources of this economy of abundance seems to have been the spiritual and moral progress which began in the midst of the Wars of Religion. Without divine help vouchsafed to the human soul, such progress would have been hardly possible. But the human will, which is free, had to seek this help, had by choice to enlist it for meeting the problems in those realms of worldly experience—religion, art and morals—for which the new scientific methods were impotent guides. Our ancestors at the time of the scientific revolution, which began at the juncture of the sixteenth and seventeenth centuries, sought to perfect the *whole* man, and not simply to improve his knowledge of the physical and biological worlds. Had these ancestors concentrated their efforts exclusively upon those sides of human experience which came within the range of the new scientific and economic thinking, the generations born in the late eighteenth and nineteenth centuries would have found it even more difficult than they did to establish the economy of abundance which had never before existed on this planet.

'There seem to be two causes of the deterioration of the arts', Socrates tells Adeimantus in *The Republic*. 'What are they?' he is asked. 'Wealth,' he says, 'and poverty.'[1] The same thing may be said also of deteriorations, and naturally of improvements, in religious and in moral conduct. In all these domains of our experience a measure of material well-being is indispensable, but, beyond a certain point, wealth is largely neutral; it strengthens some men and women and

[1] *The Republic*, IV, 421 (Jowett trans.).

weakens others. Furthermore the mere quantity of commodities measured statistically is no guide to the support which societies provide for genuine saintliness, goodness and genius in the spiritual, the moral and the artistic life.

We see that the temporal world into which the generation now in middle life was born had a spiritual, an aesthetic and a moral, as well as an economic and a scientific basis. And it is interesting to discover that the spiritual, the aesthetic and the moral, as well as the economic and scientific, basis originated in a period of war and anxiety, which is not without analogies to the age of danger in which we find ourselves today. Among the dangers that confront us, not the least is that we shall ignore the spiritual, aesthetic and moral foundations of industrial civilization. For to ignore them is certainly to refuse to follow paths which are essential to the redemption of humanity. 'Ceux qui désespèrent de mon pays devraient d'abord désespérer du monde dans lequel ils vivent, car c'est ce monde qui croule,' wrote Bernanos in 1940–1, in the shadow of the fall of France. He was speaking more for humanity than for any country. 'Nous n'avons jamais prétendu faire de ce foyer la seule maison de l'humanité....Nous avions pourtant le droit de penser qu'après l'avoir aimée et honorée, les hommes ne la délaisseraient que pour une autre plus parfaite, que ce grand effort de raison et d'amour ne serait perdu.'[1] It rests with us today to try to build this new more perfect civilization.

Our historical inquiry suggests that some of the *results* of heroic human efforts, conceived in the freedom of the mind and spirit, come generations and centuries *after* the innovations. What searchers after truth do today can hardly have immediate tangible results. Yet upon our long-range efforts the future of industrial civilization will depend, just as its existence today depended on what the human mind and spirit set about to accomplish three and a half centuries ago.

[1] 'Redevenir humain', *La Nouvelle Relève* (Sept. 1941), pp. 10–11.

Civilization and Industrialism

The future of industrial civilization in the decades and centuries which lie ahead of us is likely to depend less on the scientists, the engineers and the economists, than upon a renewal of the search for the perfection of the human personality in the mechanized and heavily administered world of our time. This search needs, as its ally, the establishment of an economy of delight, independent of the values of mass production, automation and atomic energy. It is a newly created economy of delight, in the service of the good, that should come eventually to lead and to direct the quantitative economy—the industrialism—which now dominates our planet. The qualitative resources of the human soul and of the human heart are more diverse, deeper, more inexhaustible than our contemporaries dream.

The future rests, then, with the cultivation of those sides of our nature which are, in terms of immediate productivity and success, almost entirely useless. It rests above all upon the search for and the dissemination of the many-sided truth, in which love and charity play an even greater part than justice and reason, and which the coming of Christ suggests must surely exist and must as surely be eternal. Human beings have hardly begun to recognize the possibilities for individual and social improvement which He offers them.

We have no way of knowing how long such a process of human redemption might require. We know only that with the conditions which prevail in the world today it can hardly be hoped for quickly. So we are naturally bound to reflect that, with the overwhelming power of contemporary weapons, human efforts that might civilize the world may be useless. But if total war comes *all* efforts are likely to be useless. What we need to recognize is that each time total war is avoided the need for these efforts will become more imperative, if the world is ever to live again without the threat of imminent destruction that now confronts us. That is why there is such a need to begin at once to build a society based on the spiritual resources which Christ revealed to man. What is required is a dedication, under iron self-discipline, to beauty and to truth, to charity and compassion, as well as to ethics and to justice. In working for these, it is the nature of the work, not the time required to do it, which must govern human labour. It is only by forgetting time that the great durable works of the spirit are achieved.

In the presence of transcendental truth, of beauty, of death, of love, of all that unites human beings to their Maker, it is the utilities of the terrestrial world which evaporate; it is what the terrestrial world today is prone to regard as useless that remains. 'En toute chose inutile,' Paul Valéry wrote, 'il faut être divin. Ou ne point s'en mêler.' The methods of science and technology and economics provide no key to divinity. Industrial man is not a god; his trouble is, as the late Russell Davenport has written, 'that he is not even a man'. We must find man again. That is the only way we can hope to lead him to God.

INDEX

Abélard, Peter, cited, 85, 91, 116
Adeimantus, cited, 152
'Age of the despots', cited, 128
Anselm, Saint, cited, 85
Aquinas, Saint Thomas, as expounder of the Christian faith, 32
Arabs, as keepers of careful records, noted, 26–7
Architecture, development of, 37–8, 40, 42
Archives Nationales (Paris), noted, 79 n.
Aristotle, cited, 32; use of experiments, noted, 27
Armand, Père Ignace, quoted, 100
Armour, Mrs R., cited, xiv
Art, as an aid to kindlier attitudes, 122; as an aid to science, 25; ethical content of, 110, 123, 127; nature of, 22; relation to industrialism, 107–9; separation from science, ,19, 21, 23; union of the sacred and the beautiful, 117
Artist, contrasted with scientist, 21–2; definition of, 107
Ashby, Sir Eric and Lady, cited, xii, xiii
Atrocities, change in attitude towards, 71–7, 109
Augustine, Saint, cited, 32, 73, 87

Bacon, Sir Francis, cited, 60 n., 124; importance of natural sciences to economic development, his understanding of, 61; *The New Atlantis*, noted, 60
Balzac, Guez de, cited, 123
Baro, Balthazar, secretary to marquis d'Urfé, cited, 113
Baskerville, Geoffrey, cited, 46
Bataillon, Marcel, *Erasme et l'Espagne*, noted, 81 n.
Beauvillier, duc and duchesse de, marriage of, noted, 116
Bede, Saint (The Venerable), recognized faults of the Julian calendar, 8
Benveniste, E., 'Civilisation: Contribution à l'histoire du mot', noted, 79 n.
Bernanos, Georges, cited, 2; as humanist, 1, 76; *Les grands cimetières sous la lune*, noted, 1 and 1 n.; 'Redevenir humain',

noted, 136 n. and 153 n., quoted, 136, 153,
Bernard, Saint (of Clairvaux), cited, 85, 88
Black, Joseph, cited, 63
Bodin, Jean, cited, 10, 16, 33
Boislisle, A. M. de, *Correspondance des contrôleurs généraux des finances avec les intendants des provinces*, noted, 52 n.
Book-keeping, double-entry, early development of, 14; *Jan Ympyn, Essai historique et technique sur le premier traité flamand de comptabilité*, noted, 14 n.; *Mémoire sur la Vie et les Travaux de Simon Stevin*, by Michel Steichen, noted, 14 n.
Bossuet, Jacques-Bénigne, cited, 124
Boyd, Mrs Austen T., founder of the Wiles Trust, cited, xii, xiii
Brahe, Tycho, cited, 21, 26, 27
Brémond, Henri, *Histoire littéraire du sentiment religieux en France depuis la fin des guerres de religion jusqu'à nos jours*, noted, 99 n., quoted, 99
Briggs, Asa, cited, xiii
British Museum, location of the Parthenon sculptures, brought from Greece to England by Lord Elgin, 24
Broglie, Emmanuel de, *St Vincent de Paul*, noted, 103 n.
Broglie, Victor-François, duc de, story about, 149–50
Brunelleschi, Filippo, cited, 37, 85
Buckhurst, Lord, Lord Treasurer of England under Queen Elizabeth I, concern with quantitative values, 12–14, 33
Burghley, William Cecil, Lord, Lord Treasurer of England under Queen Elizabeth I, 12
Butterfield, Herbert, *Man on His Past*, noted, ix; *Origins of Modern Science*, noted, 21, 21 n.

Calendar, correction of, noted, 27; Gregorian, established (1582–3), 9; Julian, faults of, 8, abolished, 9; Mayan, more accurate, 9

157

Index

Calendar of State Papers, Domestic, 1627–8, noted, 51 n.

Calvin, John, attitude towards art, 110, 117; quoted, 90; theories of, 87

Calvinism, austerity of, 44, 47, 90, 98, 102, 110

Capital Punishment, changes of attitude towards, 77

Carmelites, Order of, cited, 88, 90

Catholicism, *see* Church

Cellini, Benvenuto, quoted, 134

Census, first taken, 16

Cervantes, Miguel de, cited, 64, 117

Cézanne, Paul, cartoon about, noted, 22

Chablais (Savoy), example of peaceful conversion, 139–45

Chantal, Jeanne de, co-founder with Bishop of Geneva of Order of Visitation (1610), 100

Chaptal, Jean-Antoine, cited, 63

Charles I (England), cited, 49, 125, 145

Charles V (Emperor of the Holy Roman Empire), abdication of, 75; cited, 74, 81; extent of power, 70

Chartres Cathedral, cited, 24; painting of, by Corot, 22

Chaucer, Geoffrey, cited, 124

Chevalier, Jacques, editor of Pascal–Fermat letters, quoted, 31, 31 n.

Chevreuse, duc and duchesse de, marriage of, noted, 116

China, influence of Sung dynasty, 78

Church, attitude towards art, 44–5, 109–13; attitude towards war, 68–9; authority, decline in, 74; differences between Catholicism and Protestantism, 86–90; influence on economic life, 44–6, on life of the people, 81

Church of England (Anglican), comparison with Roman Catholic Church in relation to industry, 46–7

Church of Scotland (Presbyterian), attitude towards art, 46–7

Churchill, Winston, cited, 120

Civil War (England), cited, 47, 49, 51, 56, 61, 66, 134, 135

Civilization, cultural foundations, nature of, 151; definition of and development of, 79–80, 123–7; relation to industrialism, 129–39; understanding and restraint, influence of, on, 149

Coal, development of the industry, ix, 50–1; early history of industry, study of, 11–14; *Geschichte des Eisen*, by Ludwig Beck, noted, 58 n.; *The History and Description of Fossil Fuel*, by John Holland, noted, 56 n.; mines, drainage of, 57; transportation, problems of, 58

Cobban, Alfred, cited, xiii

Cœur, Jacques, cited, 129; description of his palace, 41

Colbert, Jean-Baptiste, cited, 41

Copernicus, Nicholas, cited, 18, 25, 26, 30, 33, 37, 39, 42; nature of the world, theory of, 20–1

Corneille, Pierre, cited, 118, 124, 147

Corot, Jean-Baptiste Camille, method of painting Chartres Cathedral, 22

Coryat, Thomas, *Coryat's Crudities hastily gobbled up*, noted, 146 n., quoted, 146

Council of Trent, cited, 82

Counter-Reformation, cited, 82, 90, 111

Cromwell, Thomas, cited, 44

Crusades, cruelties of, 72, 83, 103

Davenport, Russell, quoted, 155

Davenport, Mrs Russell, cited, xiv

Davy, Sir Humphry, cited, 63

Debussy, Claude, cited, 114

Defoe, Daniel, cited, 80

Dejob, Charles, *De l'influence du Concile de Trente sur la littérature et les beaux-arts chez les peuples catholiques*, noted, 111 n.

Democritus, cited, 24–5, 28, 78, 83

Desargues, Gerard, cited, 29, 64; *L'Œuvre Mathématique de G. Desargues* by René Taton, noted, 134 n.

Descartes, René, cited, 20, 28, 29, 30, 32, 48, 60, 62, 64, 67; *Discours de la Méthode*, noted, 60, quoted, 4–5

Diderot, Denis, cited, 131

Dion, Roger, cited, 17

Donne, John, cited, 123, quoted, 75

Dryden, John, cited, 124

Duplessis-Mornay, Philippe de, cited, 93

Eclipses, development of ability to predict, 30, 30 n.

Economic determinism, in Marx philosophy, 34

Economic development, differences in England and France, 48–9

Economy of abundance, explanation of, 152

Index

Economy of delight, development of, 128–30

Edict of Nantes (1598), cited, 140

Einstein, Albert, cited, 31

Elgin, Thomas Bruce, Lord, gift to British Museum of the Parthenon sculptures, 24

Elizabeth I (England), cited, 1, 3, 11, 49, 55, 93, 125

Elizabeth II (England), cited, 51

Energy, sources of, 63

England, coal-burning economy, development of, 56; free trade, benefits of, 67; industrialism, growth of, due to peace, 66–7; mass production, 53; steam engine, development of, 57

Erasmus, Desiderius, cited, 37, 39, 42, 48, 76, 82, 85, 91

Euclid, cited, 78

Evelyn, John, *Fumifugium; or the Inconveniency of the Aer and Smoke of London dissipated*, noted, 52 n., quoted, 51, 52, 56; *Sylva*, noted, 56 n.

Faith, contribution to the development of industrialism, 3–4, 19, 89, 153–5

Fanshaw, Mr (Elizabethan Customs officer), cited, 13, 16

Faraday, Michael, cited, 63

Febvre, Lucien, cited, 17; *Civilisation, le mot et l'idée*, noted, 79 n.; *Le Problème de l'incroyance*, noted, 8 n., 18 n., 39 n., 90 n., quoted, 8

Fermat, Pierre de, cited, 29, 31, 32, 64, 67; correspondence with Pascal, noted, 30; letter to, from Descartes, quoted, 4; *Œuvres de Fermat*, edited by Paul Tannery and Charles Henry, noted, 5 n.

Fernel, Jean, cited, 20, 21, 25, 28, 29, 37, 82; as one of the earliest of modern scientists, 18

Filles de la Charité, founding of order and description of their work, 100–1

Fourcroy, Antoine-François, count de, cited, 63

France, Anatole, cited, 123

Franco, Francisco, cited, 1

François I (King of France), cited, 81

Froissart, Sir John, *The Chronicles of England, France, Spain, etc.*, noted, 74 n., quoted, 73–4

Furetière, Antoine, *Le Roman bourgeois*, noted, 105 n., 112, quoted, 105

Galileo, cited, 19, 20, 28, 29, 31, 32, 48, 64, 65, 78

Gassendi, Pierre, cited, 28

Ghiberti, Lorenzo, cited, 37, 85

Gibbon, Edward, cited, x, 70, 80, 106

Gilbert, William, cited, 32, 64, 78; *De Magnete*, quoted, 27

Giraud, J. B., 'Les Épées de Rives', noted, 131 n.

Glass, changes in methods of manufacture, 52

Gobineau, Joseph A., comte de, cited, 79

Goethe, Johann Wolfgang von, story about youth of, 150

Good manners, development of, 145–6

Gregory XIII, Pope, abolished Julian calendar, 9

Hall, A. R., cited, xiii; *Ballistics in the Seventeenth Century*, 67 n.; *The Scientific Revolution*, noted, 26 n., 27 n., 31 n., 60 n., quoted, 26–7, 31

Halliman, Dr T., cited, xiii

Harvey, William, cited, 19, 28, 29, 32, 64, 65

Harzelle, Rasse de, cited, 74

Héloïse, cited, 85, 91, 116

Henry IV (France), cited, 145

Henry VII (England), cited, 43

Henry VIII (England), cited, 17, 43, 44, 49, 51, 81

Heresy, necessity of rooting it out, 92–3; non-violent method of combating it, 140–5

Herodotus, cited, x

Hippocrates, cited, 24

History, study of, as a whole, xi, xii

Hooker, Richard, cited, 84, 124

Hubble, Edwin Powell, cited, 65

Hugo, Victor, cited, 93

Humanity, *see* Civilization

Hundred Years War, story of, by Sir John Froissart, cited, 73–4

Ignatius of Loyola, Saint, cited, 103

Industrialism, bases of, 56; dependence on discoveries in science, 63; development of, 43; differences in development in France and England, 131–2; economic

Index

Industrialism (*cont.*):
  causes of, 3; effect on man's treatment of fellow-man, 77; expansion of qualitative economy, 137; genesis of, 64; goals to be sought, 153–5; mass production, 59; quality, improvement in, 129–31; quantitative economic and political thinking, relation of, 34; utility as goal of, 60; war and peace, relationship to, 66–7
Industrial Revolution, development of, 58–9; as described by Arnold Toynbee, Sen., ix
Inventions, age of, 60–1
Iron, development of, in industry, 50–3, 56
Isabella, Infanta, cited, 119

James I (England), cited, 49, 145
Jansenists, Order of, cited, 88
Jesuits, Order of, cited, 101; as missionaries, 103
John of the Cross, Saint, cited, 88, 89
John of Gaunt, quoted, 66–7
Julien, Monseigneur, St François de Sales, noted, 100 n., 103 n.

Kepler, Johannes, cited, 21, 29, 31, 32, 64, 65; correction of the mistakes of Copernicus, 26–7
Kerling, Miss Nellie, cited, xiv
Kerridge, Mr E., cited, xiii
King, Gregory, cited, 15
Koenigsberger, Dr H. G., cited, xiii
Koyré, Alexandre, 'The significance of the Newtonian Synthesis', noted, 65 n.

Labour, reduction of cost, 61
Lafayette, Madame de, La Princesse de Montpensier, noted, 118
Laffemas, Barthélemy, cited, 10
Language, The Legacy of the Middle Ages, by E. A. Lowe, noted, 124 n.; penmanship and usage, changes in, 123–7
Latimer, Hugh, cited, 124
Launoy, John de, death, story of, 73–4
Lavoisier, Antoine Laurent, cited, 63
Leblanc, Nicholas, 63
Le Bras, Gabriel, 'Canon Law', noted, 69 n.
Leclercq, Abbé Jacques, St François de Sales, noted, 91 n., 96 n., 98 n., 103 n., 104 n.

Léonard, E. G., cited, 81; Le Protestant français, noted, 81 n.
Lespine, Jean de, cited, 92, 135; Excellent discours, noted, 92 n., 95
Lipson, E., The Economic History of England, noted, 53 n.
Louis XIII (France), cited, 145
Louis XIV (France), cited, 136, 148
Luther, Martin, cited, 38, 85, 87; attitude towards art, 117; pamphlets, printing of, 38

Macaulay, Thomas B., Critical and Historical Essays, quoted, 108, 108 n.
Machiavelli, Niccolo, cited, 113; Mandragola, noted, 108, 108 n.
Magendie, M., La Politesse mondaine et les théories de l'honnêteté en France au XVIIe siècle, de 1600 à 1660, noted, 112 n., 147 n.
Magurn, Ruth Saunders, The Letters of Peter Paul Rubens, noted, 121 n.
Malestroict, Monsieur de, cited, 16
Malherbe, François de, cited, 123
Malynes, Gerard, cited, 10
Manners, John, Marquis of Granby, cited, 149
Manufacturing, development of mass production, 19, 50–4, 57, 59
Maritain, Jacques, Creative Intuition, noted, 107 n.; dedication of Cultural Foundations of Industrial Civilization to, v
Marx, Karl, cited, ix, 35
Mass Production, see Quantitative Values
Mathematics, addition and subtraction, new methods of, 17, 34; development of, 29–31; introduction of Arabic numbers, 17; logarithms, discovery of, 17; The Story of Reckoning in the Middle Ages, by Florence A. Yeldham, noted, 17 n.
Matter, structure of, 24–5, 28
Maynard, Theodore, Apostle of Charity, noted, 103 n.
Medici, Maria de, cited, 119
Mersenne, Father, cited, 4
Metals, production, increase in, 38, 44
Michelangelo, cited, 128
Microscope, invention of (c. 1580), 27
Milton, John, cited, 64, 124

Index

Mirabeau, marquis de, cited, 80; *L'Amy des Femmes ou Traité de la Civilisation*, quoted, 79; *L'Ami des Hommes ou Traité de la Population*, noted, 79

Missionary Movement, development of, 102–3

Molière, Jean-Baptiste P., *The Misanthrope*, quoted, 118

Mollat, Michel, cited, 14

Monasticism, correction of the evils of, 82; purpose of, 90; spread of, 88

Monet, Claude, cited, 114

Montaigne, Michel E. de, cited, 76, 77, 103, 123, 147; *Essais*, noted, 3 n., 113; quoted, 2–3

Montchrétien, Antoine de, cited, 10

Montemayor, Jorge de, *Diana*, noted, 112

Montesquieu, Charles de Secondat, cited, 80

More, Sir Thomas, cited, 77

Mun, Thomas, cited, 10

Mundy, Peter, quoted, 137; *The Travels of Peter Mundy in Europe and Asia*, noted, 138 n.

Napier, John, discoverer of logarithms and inventor of 'bones' for calculating, 17

National Gallery (London), 'The Horrors of War', painting by Rubens, 120 n.

Nef, Elinor Castle (Mrs John U.), x; attitude on love of fellow-man, 68; *Letters and Notes Volume I*, noted, 109 n.; *Letters* in Archives of the University of Chicago, 125 n.

Nef, John U., 'A comparison of industrial growth in France and England from 1540 to 1640', 53 n.; 'The Genesis of industrialism and of modern science', 64 n.; 'Industrial Europe at the time of the Reformation', 44 n.; 'The Industrial Revolution reconsidered', 59 n.; *Industry and Government in France and England, 1540–1640*, 47 n., 49 n., 130 n.; *La Naissance de la civilisation industrielle et le monde contemporain*, 37 n., 50 n.; 'La Riforma Protestante e l'origine della civiltà industriale', 44 n.; 'Les Causes de la guerre', 68 n.; 'Note on the progress of iron production in England', 50 n.; 'Prices and industrial capitalism in France and Eng-

land', 55 n., 60 n.; 'The progress of technology and the growth of large-scale industry in Great Britain', 60 n.; *The Rise of the British Coal Industry*, 48 n.; 'Silver production in central Europe', 38 n.; *The United States and Civilization*, 48 n.; *War and Human Progress*, 62 n., 67 n., 122 n.

Newberry Library (Chicago), noted, 144 n.

Newton, Sir Isaac, cited, 27, 31, 134

Numbers, Arabic *v.* Roman, 17; place of numbers in modern society, 7

Order of Visitation, founded (1610) by Bishop of Geneva and Jeanne de Chantal, 100

Owen, George, *Description of Pembrokeshire*, noted, 55 n., quoted, 55

Papacy, attitude towards war, 69, 71, 75; enforcement of unity, 73, 74; power of, 72

Paper, development of industry, 126; wrapping paper, manufacture of, 126 n.

Paracelsus, Philippus A., work on medicine, 20

Parthenon, marbles from, in British Museum, 24

Pascal, Blaise, cited, 5, 19, 29, 64, 65, 123, 148; correspondence with Fermat, noted, 30; *Les Pensées*, noted, 97

Peace of the Pyrenees (1659), cited, 3

Petty, Sir William, cited, 15; *The Economic Writings of Sir William Petty*, edited by C. H. Hull, noted, 16 n.

Peyrère, Isaac La, *Du Rappel des Juifs*, noted, 102 n.

Philip II (Spain), cited, 1, 43, 119, 145

Philip IV (Spain), cited, 119

Pigou, A. C., cited, 109

Pitti Gallery (Florence, Italy), 'The Horrors of War', painting by Rubens, 120

Plato, cited, 32, 83; *The Republic*, noted, 152 n., quoted, 152

Poincaré, Henri, cited, 31

Poncet, — (lawyer of Thonon), conversion of, 142

Premier et Second Avertissement des Catholiques Anglais aux François Catholiques et à la Noblesse qui suit à présent le Roy de Navarre, noted, 92 n.

Index

Printing, development of, 38–9

Protestantism, cited, 111; conversion of Chablais, 139–45; *see also* Church

Proust, Marcel, cited, 113, 123; Preface to *La Bible d'Amiens*, noted, 22 n., quoted, 22

Public Record Office (London), cited, 11, 12; Exch. K.R. Customs Accounts, 111/40, 13 n., 16 n.

Puritanism, austerity of, 46, 87, 89, 102, 110

Quaker Faith, influence of François de Sales and Vincent de Paul on, 102

Quantitative Values, development of the idea, 7, 10, 17, 33, 34, 53, 59, 62, 64, 150; quality *v.* quantity, 128–39; quantitative expansion of trade, 16, 137; relation to civilization, 153–5

Queen's University of Belfast, The (Ireland), location for delivery of Wiles Trust lectures, ix

Rabelais, François, cited, 8, 17, 37, 89, 90, 103, 111, 123

Racine, Jean, cited, 118, 131, 150

Rambouillet, Madame de, originator of the 'salon', 146

Rancé, Le Bouthillier de, founder of order of Trappists, 88

Ranke, Leopold von, *History of the Popes*, noted, 128

Réaumur, René Antoine F. de, cited, 62

Reformation, cited, 8, 37, 44, 46, 51, 56, 71, 76, 88, 92; effects of, 47–8; origins of, 81; progress of, 110–11

Religious Wars, cited, 9, 43, 152; prevalence of the idea 'to kill for Christ is the supreme virtue', 1–2; *see also* War

Rembrandt, Harmenszoon van Ryn, cited, 60, 119; 'Christ at Emmaus', 'Good Samaritan' and 'Hendriskje Stoffels', (paintings), noted, 122

Renaissance, cited, 24, 39, 42, 48, 106, 111, 128

Republic, (The) by Plato, translated by Jowett, noted, 152 n., quoted, 152

Response à un Ligueur masqué du nom de catholique anglois, par un vray Catholique bon François, noted, 94 n.

Restoration, cited, 3, 16, 134

Revolution, commercial, industrial, price, 36; in mental processes, 4–5; steps in industrial revolution, 58–62

Reynolds, Sir Joshua, cited, 149

Richelieu, Cardinal, cited, 119; 'Richelieu and Rubens', by Otto von Simson, noted, 119 n., quoted, 119

Roberts, Michael, cited, xii, xiii

Robertson, William, cited, 70, 74, 79, 80; *The History of the Reign of Charles the Fifth*, noted, 70 n., quoted, 70

Roberval, Gilles Personne, cited, 29

Robinet, Mademoiselle, cited, xiv

Rockefeller Foundation, cited, xiii

Roman Catholic Church, attitude towards war, 71–2; conversion of Chablais, 139–45; great schism, 73; influence on industry, 44–9; interest in calendar, 8; loss of power, 74–5; transfer of church properties to state, 47–8

Roman Empire, fall of, noted, 8; peace maintained, 69

Roover, Raymond de, *Jan Ympyn, Essai historique et technique sur le premier traité flamand de comptabilité*, noted, 14 n.

Rubens, Peter Paul, cited, 64, 119; 'The Horrors of War', description of painting, 120, noted, 120 n.; letter of, to Sustermans, quoted, 120–1; *The Letters of Peter Paul Rubens*, by Ruth Saunders Magurn, noted, 121 n.; 'Richelieu and Rubens', by Otto von Simson, noted, 119 n., quoted, 119

Runciman, Steven, cited, 72; *A History of the Crusades*, noted, 72 n.

Ruskin, John, *La Bible d'Amiens*, noted, 22 n.; story about Turner and Ruskin, noted, 19

Rutherford, Ernest R., cited, 31

Saint-Simon, comte de, cited, 71, 72, 116; *De la Réorganisation de la Société Européenne*, noted, 70 n., quoted, 70

Sales, François de (Bishop of Geneva), cited, 111, 114, 127, 141–4; *Controverses*, noted, 143; *Introduction to the Devout Life*, noted, 99, quoted, 96; *St François de Sales*, by Abbé Jacques Leclercq, noted, 96 n.; *St François de Sales*, by Monseigneur Julien, noted, 100 n.; *St François de Sales*, by For-

Sales (*cont.*):
tunat Strowski, noted, 95 n.; sketch of life, 94–9; *Treatise on the Love of God*, 99

'Salon', development of, 145–9

Schnabel, Artur, quoted, 105

Schrödinger, Erwin, cited, 19, 28, 65, 84; *Nature and the Greeks*, noted, 65 n., quoted, 65–6

Science, alliance with material progress, 7; applications of modern science, 63; modern science, birth of, 36; observation and experiment, as only valid proof of any scientific proposition, 27; quantitative precision, importance of, 34; scientific investigation, rise of, 18–20, 29–34; separation of science from faith and art, 4, 7, 19, 23; speeding up of scientific learning by use of new devices, 27

Scientific Revolution, causes of, 26; nature of, 31, 33; preparation for, 42; start of, 18, 34

Scott, Geoffrey, cited, 114; *The Architecture of Humanism*, noted, 114 n.

Seven Years War, cited, 149

Sévigné, Madame de, letters, noted, 113

Shakespeare, William, cited, 60, 64, 67, 124; quoted, 66–7

Sherrington, Sir Charles, cited, 19, 25, 28, 65; *The Endeavour of Jean Fernel*, noted, 29 n., quoted, 29

Sidney, Sir Philip, *Arcadia*, noted, 112

Siegfried, André, cited, xiv

Simson, Otto von, 'Richelieu and Rubens', noted, 119 n., quoted, 119

Singer, Dr Charles, *Technology and History*, noted, 63 n., quoted, 63

Smith, Adam, cited, 80

Smoke, problem of, in industry, 52

Smyth, Edward, cited, 135

Socrates, quoted, 152

Spanish Armada, cited, 8

Spanish Civil War, cited, 1

Spanish Republic, cited, 1

Spengler, Oswald, cited, 79

Spenser, Edmund, *Shepherds' Calendar*, noted, 112

State Papers Domestic, Elizabeth, CCLXVI, no. 119, noted, 55 n.

Statistics, early development of, 15; population, reports on, 15; quantitative in-formation, desire for, 7, 10; records of the coal industry, 11–14; use of, care required in, 36–7

Steam engine, development of, 57

Stendhal (pseud. of Henri Beyle), *De l'Amour*, noted, 106 n., quoted, 106

Strowski, Fortunat, *St François de Sales*, noted, 95 n., 116 n., 140–3 n.

Sung Dynasty (China), cited, 78

Sustermans, Justus, letter to, from Rubens, quoted, 120–1

Tacitus, cited, x

Tannery, Paul, *Œuvres de Fermat*, edited by Paul Tannery and Charles Henry, noted, 5 n.

Tasso, Torquato, *Aminta*, noted, 112

Taton, René, *L'Œuvre Mathématique de G. Desargues*, noted, 134 n.

Technology, rise of, 54–62

Telescope, invention of (1580), 27

Temple, R. C., *The Travels of Peter Mundy in Europe and Asia*, noted, 138 n.

Thales, prediction of an eclipse, 30 n.

Theresa, Saint, cited, 88, 90, 99, 103, 111

Thirty Years War, cited, 48, 66, 76, 145; declining prosperity during, 43

Timber, shortage of, 54–6

Tin mining, development of, 44

Titian, cited, 128

Toynbee, Arnold, Sen., theory of industrial revolution, ix

Toynbee, Arnold, cited, 79

Transportation, development of new methods, 58

Trappists, story of, 88–9

Treaty of Westphalia (1648), cited, 132

Trevor-Roper, Professor Hugh, cited, xiii

Turner, Joseph M. W., story about Ruskin and Turner, 19

Unitarianism, influence of de Sales and de Paul on, 102

Urfé, marquis d', cited, 147; *L'Astrée*, noted, 112–15, 115 n., quoted, 115

Ursulines, Order of, noted, 100–1

Valéry, Paul, quoted, 155

Vasari, Giorgio, cited, 107

Velasquez, Diego, 'The Surrender at Breda' (painting), noted, 121

Index

Vesalius, Andreas, cited, 18, 20, 21, 24, 25, 33, 42, 82
Vincent de Paul, cited, 111, 114, 127, 147; quoted, 102; sketch of, 94–102
Vinci, Leonardo da, cited, 33, 42
Visitandines, see Order of Visitation
Voltaire, François M. A. de, cited, 80
Vondel, Joost van den, cited, 124

War, attitude of church towards, 69–72; causes of, 66–8, 68 n.; definition of, 93; limitation on, 68–74; methods of, changes in, 74–6; picture of, by Rubens, 120–1; relation to industrialism, 66–7; restraints on, 150
Watts, Isaac, Sir, cited, 57, 63
Weizsächer, C. F. von, cited, 19; 'The Spirit of Natural Science', noted, 21 n., quoted, 21

Welldon, Anthony, quoted, 54–5
Whitehead, A. N., cited, 34, 65; Science and the Modern World, noted, 29 n., 30 n., 32 n., quoted, 29, 30, 32
Whittaker, Edmund Taylor, Sir, cited, 65
Wiebe, Georg, Zur Geschichte der Preisrevolution des 16. und 17. Jahrhunderts, noted, 60 n.
Wiles Trust, cited, ix, xii, 11, 35
Woman's Suffrage, story about, 37
Women, development of their influence, 103–4, 112, 114
World War I, noted, 71, 77

Yeldham, Florence, A., The Story of Reckoning in the Middle Ages, noted, 17 n.

Zwingli, Ulrich, attitude on transubstantiation, 85